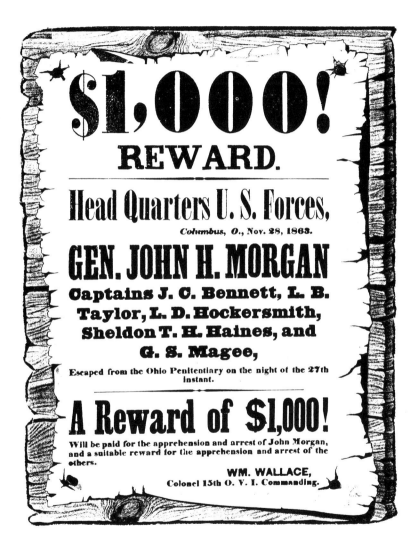

Reward Poster from the collection of Frederick P. Griffin.

Other Books in this series of
TRUE ADVENTURE STORIES FROM THE CIVIL WAR:

- **Corydon — The Forgotten Battle of The Civil War**
  By W. Fred Conway
- **The Ruthless Exploits of Admiral John Winslow —
  Naval Hero of the Civil War**
  By Paul Ditzel
- **Quantrill — The Wildest Killer of the Civil War
  and other stories**
  By Paul Ditzel

If not available at your favorite bookstore, you may order direct from the publisher at $9.95 each plus $3.00 shipping and handling.

FBH Publishers
P.O. Box 711, New Albany, IN 47151
Phone 1-800-234-1804

Library of Congress Cataloging in Publication Data
Conway, W. Fred, Sr.

The Most Incredible Prison Escape of the Civil War
Library of Congress Catalog Number: 91-070891
ISBN 0-925165-04-2

FBH Publishers, P.O. Box 711, New Albany, IN 47151-0711
© W. Fred Conway, Sr. 1991. Second edition © 1994

Typography and Layout: Pam Jones
Cover: Original etching from Century Magazine January 1891.
Enhancement, layout, color, typography by Ron Grunder

The Most
Incredible

PRISON
ESCAPE

of the Civil War

W. Fred Conway

CONTENTS

PART ONE

PART TWO

Chapter One

The Slimy Dungeon

Warden Merion of the Ohio State Penitentiary at Columbus laughed sadistically as he clanged shut the narrow iron door of the tiny damp cell. "You're here to stay," he sneered at Confederate General John Hunt Morgan, who cringed at the sudden realization that he had just been locked up for what could possibly be many years, if not for the rest of his life, in a narrow cage three feet six inches wide by seven feet long.

Earlier this day, July 30, 1863, he had been forced to strip and bathe in a wooden tub containing disinfectant, while he was scrubbed by convicts using a horse brush. His beard and mustache, as well as his long flowing hair, were shaved off until he himself looked like a convict. It was a day of humiliation for the proud general. But the sadistic warden, the potbellied Merion, was not content merely to let Morgan and his officers languish in their tiny cells - he had a dungeon deep in the prison's cellar reserved for prisoners who broke the rules, and he made sure that Morgan's men broke the rules.

No spitting tobacco juice on the floor. No dust or dirt allowed on the floor. No apple cores or peach pits on the floor. No loud talking, joking, or boisterous language. No talking during meals. No talking after lights out. No mail to be received with any comment which could be interpreted

GENERAL JOHN HUNT MORGAN

Known vicariously as "The Thunderbolt of the Confederacy" and "The Great Horse Thief", the swashbuckling Morgan was the toast of the Confederacy.

as an attack on Merion or any of his guards. Merion used excuses such as these to sentence Morgan's men to a turn in the dungeon.

The dungeon was extremely damp; there was no furniture - only a single toilet bucket - and it was infested with vermin. Major McCleary of the Morgan Raiders spent five days and nights in the dungeon, and called it "a hell on earth." He could hardly stand up when he was taken out of the dungeon, and he remembered other Morgan officers who had emerged "with their feet swollen, and blood oozing out of their fingernails and toenails." Morgan's brother, Calvin, one of the four Morgan brothers in the prison, emerged from his stay in the slimy dungeon to find himself covered with green mold.

Who *was* Brigadier General John Hunt Morgan, and why was prison Warden Merion so intent on inflicting upon him and his officers the most degrading inhuman treatment imaginable? Morgan was by now one of the most famous of the Confederate generals because of his wild adventures, exploits, and raids, which had been well publicized by the media of the time, and which read like a series of ongoing episodes of an Indiana Jones thriller. His various nicknames offer clues to his swashbuckling, flamboyant personality: "The Thunderbolt of the Confederacy", "The Great Raider", "The Great Freebooter", "The Guerrilla Chieftan", and "The King of Horse Thieves".

The six-foot-tall Morgan, a striking figure in the saddle, always wore a fresh uniform, and the plume adorning his hat set him apart. He was a charismatic leader with a magnetic personality. His men almost worshipped him. Hundreds of recruits vied for a place in his rebel army. Morgan, himself, had recruiting posters printed and circulated. He soon had

CALVIN MORGAN

Another of the four Morgan brothers in the Ohio State Penitentiary. He emerged from the dungeon covered with green mold.

over 2,000 men ready and eager to follow him anywhere, although they had no idea they would invade the North.

A recent widower, the 37-year-old Morgan could have had his choice of virtually any belle in the Confederacy. He chose pretty, vivacious 21-year-old Martha "Mattie" Ready of Murfreesboro, Tennessee. They had been married a short seven months before his capture.

Morgan made up his own military rules and regulations, devised his own battle plans, and operated virtually independently of the rest of the Confederate Army. He gave little heed to his superior officer, General Braxton Bragg, whom he detested. Likewise, Bragg lost no love on Morgan. Bragg recommended to Confederate President Jefferson Davis that Morgan be given no further promotions because his independent actions made him dangerous. Finally the feud took on such proportions that Bragg forbade Morgan to visit Mattie, who had become pregnant, shortly after their marriage. He also forbade him to cross the Ohio River to invade the North. Of course, Morgan did both.

Morgan and his band of over 2,000 Raiders caused havoc wherever they went. They wrecked Union railroad trains, blew up railroad bridges and tracks, sacked villages, towns and cities, stole horses, and demanded tens of thousands of dollars in extortion to spare stores and mills from their torches. But not one woman or child was ever molested. For all his wanton destruction, Morgan lived by a moral code.

A favorite trick was to have his personal telegrapher, "Lightning" Ellsworth, tap into telegraph lines with the telegraph key he always carried with him. With this "bug" he would send false messages to confound Union troops. Time after time Ellsworth's fake messages were swallowed hook, line, and sinker by the North, who would send troops

GENERAL ORDER.

**Head Quarters, Morgan's Cavalry,
Knoxville, August 4th, 1862.**

Soldiers:

Your country makes a fresh appeal to your Patriotism and Courage! It has been decided that Kentucky must be freed from the detested Northern yoke, and who so fit to carry out this order as yourselves?

The road is well known to you! You have already taught the Tyrants at Tompkinsville, Lebanon and Cynthiana that where Southern hearts nerve Southern arms, our Soldiers are invincible.

To an enemy be as Tigers, to our Southern brethren be as Lambs! Protect their homes, respect their property! Is it not that of your Fathers, Mothers, Sisters and Friends?

Soldiers: I feel assured that you will return with fresh laurels to enjoy in peace the fruits of your glorious victories! In the meantime, let your avenging Battle-cry be "*Butler!*" but shout "*Kentucky*" to your kindred and friends.

JOHN H. MORGAN,
Colonel Cavalry, C. S. A.

Recruiting Posters prepared by Morgan in 1862 before he had been personally promoted to Brigadier General by Confederate President Jefferson Davis. Morgan's recruiting campaign was overwhelmingly successful, as hundreds of recruits sought the privilege of serving under his command.

PROCLAMATION.

To the Inhabitants of Kentucky!

Fellow Countrymen--

I HAVE KEPT MY PROMISE.

At the head of my old companions in arms, I am once more amongst you, with God's blessing no more to leave you.

Deprived as you are by these Northern Despots of all true information respecting the War, you are propably unaware that our holy Southern cause is everywhere in the ascendant.

The so-called "Young Napoleon," McClellan, has retreated from the Peninsula. Stonewall Jackson, the 'invincible,' is asserting the superiority of our Southern Banner against the armies of Pope, Banks, Fremont, Burnside, and that of McClellan, who has joined them. His ultimate success is assured.

NO POWER ON EARTH CAN MAKE US SLAVES!

Bragg, in Tennessee, is steadily advancing with an overwhelming force on Buel, who is retreating, whilst New Orleans is on the eve of being torn from the clutches of "Butler, the infamous," and restored to its legitimate and Confederate Government.

Kirby Smith at the head of a powerful army, is already in your State, whilst Forrest, Woodward, and myself have already proven to the Yankees our existance by taking Murfreesboro, Gallatin and Clarksville, burning the railroad bridges and damaging seriously the enemy.

AROUSE, KENTUCKIANS! shake off that listless feeling which was engendered by the presence of a powerful and relentless enemy. He is no longer to be feared! We have drawn his eye-teeth! there will soon be nothing left of him but his roar!

Let the old men of Kentucky, and our noble-hearted women, arm their sons and their lovers for the fight! Better death in our sacred cause than a life of slavery!

Young men of Kentucky flock to my standard, it will always wave in the path of honor, and history will relate how you responded to my appeal, and how, by so doing, you saved your country!

JOHN H. MORGAN,

Aug. 22 1862 Col.-Commanding Brigade, C. S. A.

(MORGAN'S PRESS PRINT.)

Photo courtesy Indiana State Library

Morgan's Raiders stole a wide assortment of property in their pilfering and plundering in southern Indiana, including birdcages, calico, hams, bread, chickens and ice skates!

to capture Morgan at the reported location. Of course, he was always somewhere else.

For 25 days the dashing Morgan led his 2,000 men in a protracted raid through Kentucky, Indiana, and Ohio, comprising the deepest penetration into northern territory by any Confederate force during the entire Civil War. Chasing Morgan and his Raiders were no less than 110,000 Union troops — virtually all of the Union Cavalry in the Midwest. The Morgan Raiders were in the saddle an average of twenty-one out of every twenty-four hours, and for as long as thirty-four hours and ninety-six miles at one stretch. It was the longest organized cavalry ride in history.

When Morgan, after crossing the width of Ohio, approached the Pennsylvania border, he saw the cloud of dust stirred up by his pursuers growing ever closer and realized he could go no further. He gave the order to dismount and surrender. By the time Union Captain Burbick arrived a few minutes later, the Morgan Raiders were lying on the ground fast asleep. They couldn't even stay awake long enough to watch themselves be captured. As they slept they became prisoners of war.

Arriving shortly after the capture and taking over command from Burbick was Union General J.H. Shackleford, who immediately wrote out a message to be rushed to General Burnside:

> "Scraggsville Church - 3 miles south from Lisbon, Ohio, July 26, 1863
>
> By the blessing of Almighty God I have succeeded in capturing John H. Morgan, Colonel Cluke, and the balance of his command, amounting to 400 prisoners."
>
> J.H. Shackleford,
> Brig. Gen. Commanding

However, arriving at the surrender scene just ahead of General Shackleford was Union Major Rue, who didn't appreciate Shackleford's taking the credit. Rue, though outranked, sent his own dispatch to General Burnside, which read:

"I captured John Morgan at 2 o'clock P.M.
taking 335 prisoners, 400 horses and arms."
Major George W. Rue

Although Burnside was probably confused about who made the capture (it was actually Capt. Burbick) he knew that Morgan was finally a prisoner.

Including the cost of fielding over 110,000 militiamen sent in pursuit of Morgan, the value of 34 bridges destroyed, the demolition of 60 railroad tracks, burned warehouses and army depots, the North was out over ten million dollars, which equates to over a quarter *billion* dollars in today's money. Furthermore, Morgan's Raiders had killed or wounded over 300 Union soldiers.

Although adored by the South, Morgan was hated by the North. Warden Merion of the Ohio State Penitentiary had the opportunity to let his hatred turn into cruel punishment for the infamous Morgan and his officers, and that is exactly what he did.

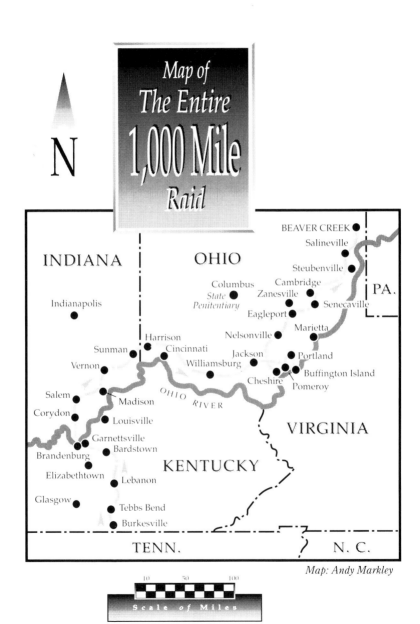

Map: Andy Markley

Chapter Two

A Letter
To Mattie

General Morgan and his officers found their new home to be a miserable collection of stone houses surrounded by both inner and outer walls. The maximum security prison was "as hot as an oven in the summer, and cold as the northern poles in winter." During August and September, the stifling heat in a building, seemingly without ventilation, was oppressive.

Morgan and his men were each locked into a 3-1/2 by 7 foot cell in the penitentiary's "East Hall" in Ranges One and Two. The cells were arranged in five tiers called ranges. Morgan's cell was in Range Two, but that of his chief scout, Capt. Thomas Hines, was Cell No. 20 in the middle of the first range, on the ground floor. Morgan's second in command, Col. Basil Duke, who was also his brother-in-law, wrote a lengthy book after the war and described the forboding old prison as follows:

> Imagine a large room, or rather a wing of a building, four hundred feet in length, forty-odd in width, and with a ceiling forty-odd feet in hight. One half of this wing, although separated from the other by no traverse wall, is called the "East Hall."
>
> In the walls of this hall are cut great windows, looking out upon one of the prison yards. If the reader will further imagine a

building erected in the interior of this hall and reaching to the ceiling, upon each side of which, and between its walls and the walls of the hall, are alleys eleven feet wide and running the entire length of the hall, and at either extremity of this building, spaces twenty feet in width - he will have conceived a just idea of that part of the prison in which General Morgan and his officers were confined. In the interior building the cells are constructed - each about three feet and a half wide and seven feet long. The doors of the cells - a certain number of which are constructed in each side of this building - open upon the alleys which have been described. At the back of each, and of couse separating the ranges of cells upon the opposite sides of the building, is a hollow space reaching from the floor to the ceiling, running the whole length of the building, and three or four feet wide. This space is left for the purpose of obtaining more thorough ventilation, and the back wall of every cell is perforated, with a hole, three or four inches in diameter, to admit the air from this passage.

We were placed in the cells constructed in that face of the building which looks toward the town. No convicts were quartered in the cells on that side, except on the extreme upper tiers, but the cells on the other side of the building were all occupied by them. The cells are some seven feet in hight, and are built in ranges, or tiers, one above the other. They are numbered range first, second, third, and so on - commencing at the lower one. The doors are grates of iron - the bars of which are about an inch and a quarter wide, and half an inch thick, and are, perhaps, two inches apart, leaving, as they are placed upright and athwart, open spaces

Morgan's brother-in-law, and second in command, Duke is remembered by historians as "one of the ablest soldiers who served the South." On June 19, 1861, he married Morgan's sister, Henrietta. Duke was a poet and an author. His book, "History of Morgan's Cavalry," written after the war in 1867, is the definitive reference on the raid. It has long been out of print. In it he describes the Ohio State Penitentiary in detail.

of two inches square between them. In front of each range of cells were balconies three feet wide, and ladders led from each one of these to the other just above it.

Duke went on to describe the revulsion of the men to the prison:

> When we entered this gloomy mansion of crime and woe, it was with misery in our hearts. There was something infernal in the gloom and the massive strength of the place which seemed to bid us to leave all hope behind. It was the stifling sense of close cramped confinement. The dead weight of the huge stone prison seemed resting on our breasts.

The prisoners were permitted to exercise during the day in the alley in front of their cells, although they were not allowed to look out of the windows. Twice a day, for breakfast (bread and molasses) and for dinner ("inferior rations"), they were herded across the yard, through the kitchen, and into a large dining hall, where they were seated at tables two feet wide.

At seven P.M. the obnoxious red-faced turnkey, "Scotty", tapped his keys on the stove, the signal for each prisoner to enter his cell, which Scotty locked, and then turned out the gaslight. Soon Morgan's men heard the steady tramp of the convicts who slept in the hall at the other end of the wing as they marched to their cells, then came the clanging shut of each cell door. Duke wrote, "When Satan receives a fresh load of prisoners, he certainly must torture each half by compelling them to hear the others locked into cells with iron doors."

The weariness of prison life gnawed at their minds and spirits. Morgan spent much of his time reading the prayer

View of Ohio State Penitentiary, Columbus.

Pretty 21-year-old "Mattie" Ready became the bride of 37-year-old John Hunt Morgan on December 14, 1862. The marriage took place in the Ready home in Murfreesboro, Tennessee, which was decorated with "holly and winterberries". The wedding feast included turkeys, hams, chickens, ducks, and "all the delicacies and good dishes of a southern kitchen." Two regimental bands provided music. They had been married only seven months when Morgan was captured. She was five months pregnant.

book Mattie had given him at their wedding. He was occasionally allowed to write letters limited to one page. On August 10th, he had been in prison eleven days, and his first letter to his young wife was allowed to be mailed:

> Having obtained the consent of the authorities, I avail myself of the opportunity of writing to you, my dearest Mattie. The day two months ago I parted from you, I thought, my dearest wife, that the separation would be for such a length of time, but, my darling, you must bear up under it, like a soldier's wife, and rest assured that as soon as I am released I shall hasten to you. I received a box of nice clothing from Mother yesterday, and today a long letter from her with a great portion of it devoted to you, my sweet wife. She said she has heard glowing accounts of you, and above all that you are a Christian. The little prayer book that you presented me upon our marriage has been my constant companion. Your picture I open often during the day and pray that the time may soon come when I may again see you. May God's blessing rest upon your head is the earnest and constant prayer of your devoted husband.

Although General Morgan had received a letter from his mother, and Basil Duke a letter from his wife, Morgan's sister, Morgan had not heard from Mattie. He was extremely worried about her, as she was now about five months pregnant. The year before Morgan had married Mattie, his first wife, Becky, had died from complications following childbirth. Could it happen again?

Two days later he was allowed to mail another single-page letter: "If I only knew that you were in good health I would be much better reconciled. I get a great number of

John Hunt Morgan's first letter to Mattie from prison. He was allowed to write only one page, and he wrote as much on it as he could.

letters from our friends in Kentucky, but I would sacrifice every pleasure and comfort to get a single line from my lovely Mattie."

Unknown to Morgan, Mattie had been writing daily. She was as worried about him as he was about her. She loved him dearly. Although Morgan never received nor read her letters, they were being received and read by Warden Merion.

Chapter Three

Inspired By Victor Hugo

One month after his incarceration, Morgan still had not heard from Mattie, so he was extremely worried. On September first, General Morgan and his brothers, Charlton, Calvin, and Richard were called into the hall. Once there, the taunting jailer, Scotty, prodded them into another room, which had an iron grating at the end. As Scotty leaned against the back wall, he motioned to the grating: "Your mother," he muttered.

Scotty would not let the four Morgan brothers speak. They could only look through the grating at their mother. She was small, weak, and sick, but she had insisted on making the trip from her home in Lexington, Kentucky, to see her boys. No words were allowed. After a minute of looking through the grating, Scotty began to curse and shout obscenities at the frail mother, who was visibly shaken by the sight of her four boys in prison. A fifth son, 18-year-old Tom, had been killed during the raid, about two weeks before his brothers were captured. Charlton Morgan recorded in his diary, "May God some day smite him [Scotty] with His wrath and make him realize in the torturing of his mind his own inhumility."

Two weeks after his mother's visit Morgan had still not heard from Mattie. On September 13th he wrote his fifteenth one-page letter to her:

General Morgan, as a child, in his mother's arms. It was this lady, some 35 years after this painting was made, who came to see her four boys in prison. A fifth son had been killed several weeks earlier, and a sixth son was too young to serve. Her daughter, Henrietta's husband, Basil Duke, was in the prison also.

The boyhood home of John Morgan on Tate's Creek near Lexington, Kentucky.

Morgan's mother had journeyed from this home in Lexington, Kentucky, to visit her sons in prison. She could only look at them through the bars while the guard swore at her.

CHARLTON MORGAN

The four Morgan brothers could only look at their frail mother through the grating as prison guard Scotty swore at her. Chalton wrote in his diary, "May God someday smite him [Scotty] with His wrath."

RICHARD MORGAN

Of John Hunt Morgan's four brothers who accompanied him on the raid, it was Richard who was made a colonel and given a cavalry unit to command. He injured a leg in the raid, and traded his cell so his brother John could escape.

Another week has passed, my darling wife, without anything from you. I look eagerly forward to each day to bring a sweet missive, but it is almost hoping against hope, for I am aware of the great difficulty of getting letters through. I have written you fourteen.

It would be useless, my darling Mattie, to describe the great pain that this lengthened separation from you gives me, and but for the consolation that hope affords, I would indeed be most miserable. But you know, my beautiful one, that by nature I am blessed with good spirits and look at the bright side of everything. But for the uncertainty of your condition, I could bear this incarceration with a much greater degree of stoicism. Farewell my darling, ten thousand blessings accompany this. Think of me often and know that my entire devotion and love are all yours.

On September 16th, Scotty handed him an envelope. It was addressed to him in Mattie's handwriting! His heart leaped for joy. As Scotty snorted, Morgan saw that the envelope was empty. Suddenly he knew. He knew that Mattie's letters were being withheld from him. Somehow he had to get out of prison to see if she was all right. However, two men in the prison knew how Mattie was getting along. From her letters, Warden Merion and jailer Scotty knew Mattie was very sick.

Morgan's impatience at his galling confinement, his anger at being unable to speak to his mother, and now his frustration over Mattie's letters being withheld from him, which kept him from knowing whether she was well, all began to tell on him. He grew restless, and he resolved to escape at any price.

While Morgan chafed, read the prayer book Mattie had given him, and continued to write to her as often as he was permitted, Morgan's officers tried to pass the time by playing cards and chess or by reading books. Basil Duke even whiled away the hours by writing poetry. One of his poems, though not likely to win any prize, has survived:

The Rebel's Dream

At midnight in his grated cell
Bright visions to the captive came
He dreams his time of stay is done.
His dungeon doors are open thrown
He dreams that "Jeff" at last relents
To slacken up and straight consent
And by some apt negotiation
Redeem him from the Yankee nation.
The raider dreams that he rides again
In battle's stern parade.
But his dream is rudely shattered when -
Upon his awakened hearing jars
The clash of those detested bars.
He hears his jailer's sullen tones
That makes King Merion's mandate known
And bids him right away prepare
To lose his cherished beard and hair.

Toward the end of October the prisoners were allowed to purchase books from the prison library. One book had not sold. It was a new book by the celebrated French novelist Victor Hugo, best known for his "Hunchback of Notre Dame." His newest book was entitled "Les Miserables". It hadn't sold because it was written in French, and no one could read it. No one, except Captain Thomas Hines, who was more than a Confederate scout and spy; he was a former college professor, and he both spoke and wrote fluently in French. With his last silver coins he bought the book.

In this new French novel, the hero, Jean Valjean, repeatedly escaped from prison using clever and ingenious methods. The more he read of Valjean's exploits, the stronger grew Hines' desire to formulate an escape plan of his own. As he sat there in his cell, on the edge of his cot with the book in his lap, he stared down at the floor. Suddenly he straightened up, letting the book slide from his lap as he kept looking down. Comprehension began to flicker in his eyes when a peculiarity about his cell dawned on him. The floor was completely dry in a cell where it should be wet because the walls were always damp and the ceiling continually dripped moisture; yet, the floor was *dry*. To any other prisoner this might have had little meaning, but to the astute Hines it could mean but one thing — the concrete floor of his cell must not be in contact with the ground! *There had to be an air space beneath the floor.* Given this set of circumstances, what would Victor Hugo's Valjean do?

The "Jeff" referred to in Duke's poem, "The Rebel's Dream" was Jefferson Davis, President of the Confederate States of America.

Chapter Four

Through
The Floor

Quickly Hines grabbed the wooden prop under his bed and thumped on the floor of his cell. Yes, it sounded hollow!

Scotty's assistant jailer was a deputy warden called "Old Hevay". Unlike Scotty, Hevay was kindhearted, and he knew a great deal about the formidable old penitentiary. He had often commented about its architectural grandeur. Impatiently, Hines waited until Hevay walked by on his rounds.

"Say, Hevay," Hines began. "You know all about this prison, do you not?" "A little, maybe," Hevay replied, wondering what Hines was getting at. "There's got to be some reason the floor of my cell is dry, when the rest of the cell is wet. I figured if anyone would know, why it would be you." Old Hevay, obviously proud that his knowledge was being tested, and anxious to impress Hines, couldn't resist the temptation to reveal what he knew about the prison's construction. "Sure, there's a tunnel runs right under the cells on Range One for the air that goes to the ceiling." Hines contained his excitement well. Old Hevay continued his rounds, never suspecting that Hines' mind was already at work on a plan of escape.

It didn't take Hines long to share his idea with Morgan, who jumped at the possibility that this could be the miracle they had been praying for. Five more of Morgan's officers on

Range One were entrusted with the secret: Captain Taylor, another Morgan scout and a nephew of former President Zachary Taylor; Capt. Hockersmith, a stonemason by profession; and Captains Bennett, Sheldon, and Magee. They decided to start a hole under Hines' cot in his Cell No. 20. They would need tools.

The knives from the prison dining room did not have pointed ends, for obvious reasons. This meant their squared end would make excellent chisels. Hines knew that two of the officers in Range Two were sick and would have their meals brought to their cells. When the trays were returned to the kitchen, the knives kept behind were not missed.

On November 2nd*, with Hines seated on the edge of his cot acting as lookout, Hockersmith and Taylor began digging, alternating every other hour. Hines pretended to read his book, but he was alert to give a prearranged signal if Scotty or Old Hevay approached. One tap on the floor with the bed prop meant to dig; two taps - stop; three taps - danger, come out immediately. In case the digging made enough noise to cause concern, Hines would start to sing, "The Old Cow Crossed The Road" or "Grasshopper Sittin' On A Tater' Vine," and others would join in.

Unknown to Morgan and Hines and all the others, on the very day the digging began, daily inspection of the cells was discontinued. A letter Morgan had written several days earlier had done the trick. Scotty and Hevay had been relieved of guard duty in the East Hall, and their replacements had no desire to inspect or sweep the prisoners' cells. It was almost too good to be true!

On Friday, October 31st Morgan had written a letter to General John S. Mason, Commander of Camp Chase, the

---

* Some accounts place the date on November 4th.

The Filson Club

CAPTAIN THOMAS HENRY HINES

Described as "shifty-eyed," "wily," and "sly," Hines was the mastermind behind the escape. Historians later called him "the most dangerous man in the Confederacy."

military prison in Columbus. Mason was the officer in charge of the soldiers who were supposed to be guarding the prisoners of war in the State Penitentiary. These soldiers, Morgan insisted, were not doing their job and were letting the regular prison guards mistreat them. Morgan demanded that Mason's soldiers obey international law regarding prisoners of war and assume the duty of guarding them so that they would be treated as prisoners of war and not as common convicts subject to the insolent, sadistic treatment they were enduring. No one was more surprised than Morgan when his letter produced immediate results. General Mason called a meeting with Warden Merion and his prison board of directors. They quickly agreed that, in accordance with international law, Morgan's officers would be guarded only by Union soldiers.

Neighboring Camp Chase would send a 27-man guard detail each day to watch the prisoners, after they were let out of their cells for the day. Two of the soldiers were to be stationed in the hallway of the cellblock, and the others would patrol the yard outside the building. After the prisoners were locked back in their cells for the night, the Union soldiers would march back to Camp Chase.

One of General Mason's officers assigned to the guarding detail, Lt. Mark W. Goss, asked who would sweep out the cells. "Let the rebels do it themselves," was Mason's quick reply. That seemingly insignificant decision paved the way for the undetected removal of chipped concrete, mortar, and brick from the growing hole under Hines' cot. Hines, apparently resolving to become a model prisoner, often swept out his cell during the day.

Although the soldiers patrolled the alley, the cells themselves never again were inspected. And the soldiers never questioned the prisoners who went in and out of Cell

No. 20, although their visits occurred more frequently than might ordinarily be expected. Cards, chess, casual visits — nobody cared. Yet, Hines was always ready to tap or sing if the need arose.

The two stolen knives were made of soft iron, and the chipping went slowly. Hockersmith recorded in his diary, "My recollection is that we worked all day, but that night we could scarcely tell what had been done. The concrete proved to be harder than ordinary rock. Consequently, Capt. Sam Taylor had not much more than his vest pocket full of rubbish to dispose of."

During this first day of digging, Morgan wrote the last letter that Mattie was to receive from him while he was in prison. A relative had sent him a bouquet of violets. He pressed them into the letter. "These were sent to me by Miss Sally Warfield. I send them to you, dearest." He still had no way of knowing that she was gravely ill: "My love, know, dearest, you are first and last in all the prayers of your devoted husband. If I can hear from you and that you are still blessed with health, then I can be as seeming happy as any." But Morgan did *not* hear. He agonizingly monitored the activity in Cell No. 20.

As the flat-end knives broke apart from constant use, they were replaced by more knives other ailing prisoners forgot to return with their food trays. Still the knives were not missed. Then another breakthrough occurred. Incredible as it seems, the prisoners were actually allowed to purchase tiny saws! Many northern prison camps allowed rebel prisoners to fashion rings, and pins from bones, shells, and buttons. Morgan's men actually were allowed to purchase three watchspring saws with 35 blades!

The constant chipping under Hines' cot produced fragments of concrete, which were hidden in handkerchiefs and in pockets, and then placed in an old carpet bag Hines had swapped with another prisoner for a pair of socks.

The cell floor consisted of three inches of cement on top of a five inch bed of lime mortar. These two layers were on top of a brick arch covering the air chamber. The arch itself was constructed of three layers of brick 18 inches thick. From the floor under Hines' cot down into the air chamber was a total of 26 inches of masonary - cement, mortar, and brick. The knives, along with the tiny saws, slowly made progress through layer after layer of the old masonary construction.

On November the third, the second day of digging, Bennett and Magee took turns under the cot. Taylor's and Hockersmith's hands were too sore from chipping the concrete the previous day. Hockersmith recorded in his diary, "Hines insisted that each man take a turn of not more than an hour because the soldiers were familiar with their faces, and if they didn't see a man about in the hall, they made it a practice to walk down the row of cells and inquire after him."

On the third day, with Hockersmith again taking over for an hour under the cot, one of the guards sensed his absence. "Where's Hockersmith?" he wanted to know. Morgan answered quickly, "I left him lying on my bed a few minutes ago not feeling well." "Let's go up to your cell and see if he's there or not," the guard snarled as he followed Morgan up the ladder to his cell on the second tier - Range Two.

While they climbed the ladder, Hockersmith scooted out from under the cot in Cell 20, slipped into his own cell, also on the first tier, and covered himself with a blanket. When the guard, Milo Scott, found Morgan's cell empty, he scurried back down the ladder looking for Hockersmith on

*Courtesy, Department of Photography,
Ohio State University*

An actual photograph of Ranges One and Two, with Ranges Three and Four visible at the upper left.

the ground floor. There he found him, moaning with a feigned illness under his blanket on the cot in his own cell. Hockersmith continued the deception by pretending to be sick for another two days.

Whenever the suspicious Milo Scott asked the whereabouts of any of the men who were doing the digging, Morgan engaged him in conversation, sometimes by asking his opinion on the progress of the war. Scott, flattered that the great General would ask his opinion, always stopped to converse with Morgan, which gave the man in question time to slip out of Cell 20, in response to Hines' three taps, and to appear in the alley or in his own cell. The naive Scott never caught on.

The third day of chipping away at the masonary produced good progress. A hole about 14 inches in diameter had been gouged out of the floor. However the fourth day of digging generated such excitement among the prisoners that they contained themselves with difficulty. That day Bennett and Sheldon had alternated on the first shift; Taylor and Magee on the second; and, finally, Hockersmith, pretending to have recovered from his feigned illness, took over. His knife found a weak spot in the mortar between the bricks and slipped. He worked the knife back and forth. It moved easily. He worked the knife sideways. The old brick moved. He lifted it out. The damp, cool air which greeted his face left no doubt that he had penetrated the floor all the way through to the air tunnel. Then ever so easy he dropped the brick into the hole. The time it took before he heard it land on the damp earth below told him the air chamber had to be several feet high. He wanted to let out a hoop of joy, but he simply crawled out from under the cot, looked at Hines who pretended to read as he sat on the edge of the cot, and mouthed the words, "We're through the floor!"

Chapter Five

Through The Granite Foundation

News of the breakthrough was speedily relayed to Morgan's ears. He gave his congratulations to all involved and then managed to get with Hines for a conference. It was decided that Hines himself, being small and slender, would descend through the hole into the tunnel rather than Hockersmith who was heavyset, although Hockersmith's mason's skills could have given him an advantage. Hines played sick and refused his dinner. While the others marched out to the dining hall, Hines remained in his cell and gingerly lowered himself through the newly excavated opening beneath his cot. His feet touched the soft earth, and, prepared as always, he took a candle from his pocket and lit it. He was in a tunnel about five feet high and twenty feet long.

The foundation of the building appeared to be made of granite, not an easy material to penetrate. He chipped at the foundation mortar with his knife. It crumbled. He again used the knife to probe the dirt floor. It was soft. Obviously there were two choices: somehow go through the granite foundation or dig *under* the granite making a tunnel lower than the one in which he was stooping. The last choice would bring them into the jail yard, between the inner and the outer walls of the prison.

Deferring to professional judgment, he decided to get Hockersmith's opinion. Who would know better how to proceed than a trained stone and brick mason? When the others returned from dinner, Hines was grinning. "Hockersmith's got to go down. He'll know what to do next," Hines whispered to Morgan. "Tomorrow," Morgan replied.

Before Cell No. 20 was locked for the night, Hines had managed to dump a bed full of concrete chips into the hole. His bed was now smooth again for the first time in four days. He had called his lumpy bed of hidden masonary fragments a "Hindu torture platform." But this night he slept well.

The next day, November 6th, Hockersmith enlarged the hole and lowered himself into the air chamber. At the far end, he found a small, boarded up grillwork, but no daylight showed through the slats. Why not? On the other side of the grill should have been the prison yard. Something on the outside had to be blocking the grill. "I can find out," Hines responded after Hockersmith had emerged from the hole and reported the problem. True to his word, Hines found a way to get his answer. He requested permission for the men to wash their clothes in a trough in the prison yard. Permission was granted, and Hines and Hockersmith carried their dirty clothes across the yard and over to the trough. Hines washed and scrubbed shirts, drawers, and pants, while Hockersmith hung them out to dry. Hockersmith, strolling around as if looking for the best drying space, approached the spot where he calculated the grill to be. No wonder the sunlight couldn't get through. There was a big coal pile - about 40 bushels - against the wall. This eliminated any plans to escape through the grate. If it were removed, the coal would pour into the tunnel. They would have to use the option of continuing the tunnel right *through* the granite foundation. But what direction should they go? Where would they come out? How would they dig?

Hindered, but undaunted, the clever and ingenious

A view of the Ohio Penitentiary showing the prison yard.

group, General John Hunt Morgan and his officers, soon made new plans. On the morning of November 7th, as they were washing in the wooden trough in the jail yard, Hines spied a small rusty shovel with a broken handle. He passed this bit of information to the others. Now, horseplay in the yard was considered good exercise by the jailers, so the prisoners were permitted to wrestle, play leap-frog, and generally push and shove each other around in a friendly display of frustration, boredom, and unspent energy. Somehow the horseplay became concentrated in the area of the old shovel. On this chilly November day, Capt. Bennett fortuitously had worn his heavy army overcoat. Where else should the shovel end up but under his coat? The guards suspected nothing. This was the way the shovel traveled to the air chamber, where it lay ready to help breech the wall and tunnel beyond it.

Next, they needed to know the direction the tunnel should take once the wall was penetrated. Relating the site of their building to the prison yard was vitally important, but the windows were too high to afford a view, even for those housed in Range Two. This time Capt. Taylor's agile brain came up with a plan. Being short, athletic, and of powerful build, he placed a bet with his guard that, without using his feet on the ladder, he could go hand over hand up the ladder used for cleaning the ceiling. The bet was on. As Taylor easily pulled himself up the ladder, using only his hands, he was able to look out of the window and quickly survey the prison yard. Mentally, he made a map which decided the direction the tunnel should take.

Next, the question arose as to how *long* the tunnel should be. The ever resourceful Hines was ready to find out. It was easy for him to provoke a guard into an argument about the length of the hall. To prove Hines was wrong, the gullible guard actually got a measuring line and gave Hines

View of the "alley" with Ranges One and Two.
Range Three is visible above Range Two. Note
the high windows at the right.

the true length of the hall. The guard was right, and Hines was wrong.

On November 8th, 9th, and 10th, the men chiseled away at the granite foundation of the jail building. It was tough work. Taylor's hands bled where they were rubbed raw from the handle of the iron knife. Hockersmith, Sheldon, Bennett, and Magee each worked an hour at a time. Hines never left his cell, staying ready to tap the post or to break out in song about the cow or the grasshopper if the men in the tunnel were in any danger. Often he would talk to a guard, right in his cell, about the adventures of Jean Valjean or some aspect of another book he was reading, such as Gibbons' "Rise And Fall Of The Roman Empire."

Finally, after three more days of trying to chisel the big granite block loose, it budged. It took three of them, Taylor, Bennett, and Hockersmith to pull it into the hole. November 13th marked the finish of their struggle through the foundation wall. They had located the air chamber by digging through concrete, bricks and mortar; they had managed to dislodge a granite block after days of grueling work, but each obstacle only fired their determination to be free. The same afternoon, keeping a map of the yard in their heads, they started tunneling under the jailyard.

The thirteenth turned out to be momentous in another way. Morgan received a parcel. Alas, it was not from Mattie, but it was important nevertheless. Warden Merion had to have accumulated quite a collection of letters and parcels from Mattie by this time. Instead of communication with his wife, which wouldn't have reached him, anyway, this package was from his sister, Henrietta, who was married to Basil Duke. Curious and excited, he wondered what could it be? It was a Bible! He was happy about his sister's thoughtfulness. He could read all the Scriptures, not just those in his treasured prayer book from Mattie. But as he sat on his cot

Courtesy, Ohio State University

A view of the front of the Ohio Penitentiary.

examining the Bible, he began to wonder if Henrietta might have had some special purpose in sending it, other than his spiritual enrichment. He opened it to the page with the ribbon marker. Scrutinizing each line, his eye saw a tiny ink dot next to the verse, "The last shall be first, and the first shall be last." With one of the spare knives he had stolen from the dining room, he slit open the inside of the back cover. There were five Federal "greenbacks" — one hundred dollar bills hidden there. Then he slit open the front cover. Five more hundred dollar bills were tucked inside it. Morgan *had* to get out of prison to check on Mattie. She was now eight months pregnant. He was sick with worry for her wellbeing. But his predicament was one of the worst. His cell was on Range Two floor, while the hole to the tunnel was on the ground floor in Cell 20, Range One. He must form a plan to exchange cells with one of his men on Range One. His desperation to get out drove his mind to plan, plan, plan.

The fact was, there was only *one* hole into the tunnel — from Hines' Cell 20. But seven of them had been in on the

53

plan from the beginning. All had worked until their fingers had bled. The solution finally presented was to dig from the air chamber up *under* the cells of *each* of the men until there were seven holes 25 inches deep, which would leave only one inch of concrete floor to penetrate easily at the appropriate time. This way each man would have his own private hole under his cot through which he could enter the tunnel from his locked cell.

But Hines, the mastermind of the escape, had another worry. When they broke through the tunnel at the edge of the yard, they would still not be out of the Ohio State Penitentiary. The outer wall, twenty-five feet high, loomed as a last barrier. Could they hurdle this final obstacle to their freedom, or would their fascile minds not be able to cope with another challenge? If someone hatched a good idea, would they make it work?

Chapter Six

"Tonight!"

While Morgan schemed how to escape so that he could be with her, Mattie was miserable. She suffered knowing her husband was in prison; she was having trouble carrying their baby; and the war was not going well for the South. General Robert E. Lee had been dealt a crushing defeat at Gettysburg; Vicksburg had fallen; and Tennessee could be overrun by the North if Chattanooga were to fall, which was now much more than a remote possibility.

A friend of Mattie's had a home in Danville, Virginia, near the North Carolina border. South of Richmond, about 125 miles, it would later become the capital of the Confederacy, where her husband would report after his release. Feeling she would be safer there, and without her husband to advise her, she did what seemed best and took the train to Danville. It was a long arduous trip, with many changes and inevitable layovers. But before she could recover from the rigors of the trip, she was hit with shocking and depressing news.

Her brother-in-law, 18-year-old Tom Morgan, had been killed in Kentucky. His last words as he died in his brother Calvin's arms had been, "Brother Cally, they have killed me." He had been a lieutenant in John's cavalry and had been leading a squad of men in storming a railroad station occupied by Union troops. A Union bullet had found its

THOMAS MORGAN

The youngest of the Morgan brothers on the raid, Tom's friendly demeanor and clear tenor singing voice endeared him to the men. His brother John's favorite, he was the first of the brothers to lose his life for the Confederate cause. He was just 18 years of age. When Mattie arrived at Danville, Virginia, she learned that Tom had been killed, and that her brother Horace had been wounded.

mark. Tom had been her husband's favorite. They all loved the gentle young man with the sweet tenor voice.

But that wasn't all the bad news. A casualty list had just been issued showing her brother, Lt. Horace Ready as wounded. "Dear Brother!" she sobbed, burying her face in her hands.

As Mattie's strength of spirit returned somewhat, she resolved to obtain her husband's release. She began to write letters - to Confederate Secretary of War James Seddon, to Colonel Robert Ould of the Prison Exchange Commission, and to Colonel Johnston, all in Richmond. She begged them to effect an exchange of her husband for Union General Neal Dow, who was being held in a Confederate prison. But the Confederate government turned a deaf ear.

Not deterred, Mattie wrote directly to Union President Abraham Lincoln in Washington, imploring him to exchange her husband for General Dow. Lincoln received her letter, read it, and passed it on to Secretary of War Stanton for possible action. Mattie, whose troublesome pregnancy was keeping her confined to her bed, waited days, weeks, and then months for a reply.

While Mattie was doing everything she knew to free her husband, work on the escape was progressing at the prison. Hockersmith, the stone mason, was chosen to begin digging the tunnel. The first day he moved forward one-and-a-half feet. He used shirts as bags to pull the dirt from the tunnel leading off from the air chamber. The next day he struck hard tough clay, which broke one of the knives. Always resourceful, Hines conveniently produced a straight razor. He possessed an amazing ability to come up with whatever was needed, whenever it was needed. Historians would one day term him "the most dangerous man in the Confederacy."

Union President Abraham Lincoln, to whom Mattie wrote imploring him to exchange her husband for captured Union general Neal Dow, who was in Libby Prison in Richmond. Lincoln read her letter, and turned it over to Secretary of War Stanton for action. He refused to exchange her "noble" husband.

The tunnel lengthened an inch at a time, and by November 16th, Hockersmith's hands were so cramped from holding the razor that he could not continue, and work stopped for the day.

Bennett took over the following day, but his hands soon became so blistered he could not continue. Next, Taylor tackled the tunnel with the razor, which was still intact. To aid in excavating the dirt, a small wooden box, which Taylor had found and smuggled into his cell was used, after he had cut a hole in one end with the razor. The box was passed along to Hines' cell, where it disappeared down the hole, making its way along 20 feet of air chamber, then into the tunnel, which was now five feet long. A bed prop pushed the box into the tunnel, where the digger would fill it with dirt and clay. Back in the air chamber, a second man, using a rope made of bed ticking, would pull out the box, empty it, and shove it back into the tunnel for another load. On November 18th they had already dug a tunnel 12 feet long, three feet high, and 18 inches wide. To illuminate their work in the dark passage, they used up nine pounds of candles which they had hoarded.

On Thanksgiving morning, the tunnel was nearly completed. Hockersmith drove a wire through the remaining foot of earth and saw daylight! Work was suspended on extending it to its full length so that time could be used to make the escape holes, which were carved and chipped up through the roof of the air chamber, coming out under each of the seven cells, which left only a single inch of cement between the cell floor and the air chamber below.

Morgan was preoccupied with leaving the prison at the earliest possible moment, and he had not been idle. He had braided a stout rope from his bed ticking, which could hold the weight of a man. Every three feet he had braided in a "climbing loop." To get the rope over the 25 foot outer prison wall, he had bent an old poker into the shape of a hook.

When November 27th arrived, seven escape holes, covered by seven cots in seven cells on Range One, were ready. The tunnel from the air chamber, below, up into the prison yard was completed except for the final few inches of dirt, which were loosened and ready to give way.

Morgan's brother, Richard, who was still lame from an injury suffered more than four months earlier during the raid, occupied Cell No. 21 next to Hines. He gladly volunteered to exchange his cell for that of his famous brother the night of the escape.

November 27th turned out to be the most momentous day, yet, in the lives of the prisoners. The former guard, the kindhearted "Old Hevay", appeared at Morgan's cell and handed him the letter he had waited four months to receive. *It was from Mattie!* She was in *Danville, Virginia!* What on earth was she doing *there?*

At about the same time Morgan got Mattie's letter, Mattie herself received the letter she had been hoping and praying for, but its contents sent her into uncontrolable bursts of weeping and sobbing. It was from Col. Johnston at the Confederate capitol at Richmond.

> "I am confident they would never agree to exchange your noble husband for any general of theirs whom we now have or may hereafter capture. They think him too great a prize and dread him too much in his liberated future."

Lincoln had given Mattie's letter to Stanton, who in turn had given it to General Halleck. It was Halleck's decision that Dow was not to be exchanged for Morgan, who was to be kept in maximum security in the Ohio Penitentiary.

Mattie's friends heard her sobbing and rushed to her room, but could not calm her. A doctor was summoned. "Her time is here," he announced after examining Mattie. "Her grief has started her labor."

Incredible events were still happening that eventful day of November 27th. Morgan learned from the Camp Chase soldier guarding him that General Mason was being transferred the next day. "Undoubtedly the new commandant will order an inspection of all facilities under his control" Morgan reasoned. Even the most casual inspection of the cells easily would reveal the escape plan. The tunnel had been completed not one day too soon. Even though Morgan had wanted to wait for a warmer day, lest the rain turn to snow and leave their tracks, he knew now there could be no delay. He spread the word: *"Tonight!"*

Chapter Seven

Over
The Wall

The countdown to the escape had begun. Morgan and Hines, who had agreed to stick together once over the prison wall, timed the escape to begin at ten minutes past midnight. That would give the guard time to finish his midnight bed check and would also put them over the wall in time to find their way to the nearby Little Miami Railroad Station, where they would take the night express to Cincinnati.

Each of the seven escapees had received packages of civilian clothing from home, which they were permitted to wear after their Confederate uniforms had worn out. But the tattered uniforms would still serve one last vital purpose. They would be used to encase rolls of bed clothing, making dummies which would be left in their cots to fool the guard.

Trying to be nonchalant at dinnertime was not easy. The seven men not only cleaned their plates, but they also ate extra portions offered by other of Morgan's officers who would not attempt the escape. They wished to fortify themselves for the time they might have to wait until they could safely seek food as they fled.

After returning to the cellblock, the men waited for the tap of the jailer's keys on the stove, the signal to go to their cells for the night. At seven o'clock the keys tapped as usual, but Dick Morgan, instead of climbing the ladder to his cell, entered his brother John's cell on the second tier. John Morgan entered Dick's cell, number 21, next to Hines on the first floor, and they both got into bed, turned their heads toward the wall, pulled the coverlets over their heads and pretended to fall asleep. But sleep they did not.

Their hearts were pounding as they began what was probably the longest five hours and ten minutes of their lives. The prison bell tolled the hours: eight o'clock ... nine o'clock ... ten o'clock ... eleven o'clock. Each time the bell tolled, the guard made his rounds, lantern in hand, peering into the dark shadows of the cells to account for all the prisoners. Five of the men made sure the guard could see their faces, but John and Dick Morgan, in the wrong cells, kept their faces turned away from their cell doors, using their blankets to hide the contour of their faces. At last the prison bell clanged twelve strokes. Midnight. Ten minutes left to pass until they would attempt the most incredible prison escape of the Civil War.

The glow of the guard's kerosene lantern got brighter, then faded and disappeared. Still they waited. Would he suspect something and return? All was quiet. When Captain Taylor figured it was ten minutes after midnight, he got out of his bunk, rolled his old uniform around some bed clothes to form a dummy, placed it under the coverlet, reached his leg under the cot and stomped hard with his boot heel. The thin layer of concrete floor gave way, and Taylor lowered himself through the opening down into the air chamber. The six others followed the same procedure, except for Hines, who paused long enough to leave a note on top of his pillow under his blanket. With Hockersmith in the lead, the seven men groped their way through the air chamber and into the tunnel. Total darkness engulfed them, for they dared not light a candle. They knew their way well enough; after all, they had made the tunnel inch by inch.

The arrow shows the point that the escape tunnel opened into the prison yard. The 25 foot high outer wall they would have to scale is at the left.

They had to crawl along the three foot high tunnel, and when Hockersmith reached the end, he used the trusty razor to cut through the final few inches of dirt and sod. In another moment Hockersmith was in the prison yard, unnoticed. No one looked, no dogs barked, and the rain had not turned to snow. The cold drizzle kept the dogs inside their dry kennels. Six more men emerged from the tunnel into the cold, rainy November night.

Captain Taylor, the most athletic of the men, had been chosen to toss the hooked rope over the brick coping of the outer wall. As it hit the bricks, the noise sounded loud enough to alert the guards, but there was no response. The guards were gathered around a small fire warming themselves. Their conversation and the crackling of the flames had prevented their hearing the bent-poker hook striking the brick masonary.

If even one of the men were to successfully escape, it must be General John Morgan. He was first to climb the rope he had braided. It held. As he prepared to lower himself down the outside of the wall to freedom, his fingers touched a thin rope stretched along the outer edge on top of the wall. He knew immediately what it was, for as a boy in Kentucky, he had used a similar setup with his rabbit snares. This was obviously a tripping device connected to a bell in the warden's office. Gently he cut the rope and slowly released the tension. No alarm sounded. One by one each of the men climbed and then descended the 25 foot outer prison wall.

They tried to shake the rope loose, but Taylor had anchored it well; it wouldn't budge. The only choice was to leave it. The men shook hands, wished each other well, and went their separate ways. Morgan and Hines started to walk toward the railroad station.

Not knowing exactly where it was, when they spotted railroad tracks, they followed them to the Little Miami depot. Few people were in the station at that time of night. Hines purchased two tickets for Cincinnati, while Morgan kept his back to the waiting passengers.

The railroad conductor, W.H. Eckert, was on the platform supervising the makeup of the night express to Cincinnati. He later testified that two men, appearing to be cattle drovers, stepped up to him about one o'clock a.m. and asked

An artist's conception of the men going over the wall, from the January 1891 issue of Century Magazine.

when the train would pull out. He replied it would leave on time - in twenty more minutes. Morgan and Hines decided not to sit together. As Morgan entered the passenger coach, he saw a Union officer and sat down beside him, thinking he would be less open to suspicion. Morgan engaged him in casual conversation, and as the train moved forward, the wall of the penitentiary loomed ahead. Noticing it, the Union officer remarked, "That is the hotel at which Morgan stops, I believe." "Yes," replied Morgan. "He will not be released.

May he ever be as closely kept as he is now."

The train stopped at Xenia, and Hines jumped off to chat with the telegraph operator. The operator showed no excitement, and obviously had not received any wire about a prison escape. Their flight had not yet been discovered. Near Dayton, the train ground to a stop. Fearing the worst, Morgan and Hines moved into the vestibule, ready to jump into the night if necessary. However, the stop had been caused by an obstruction on the tracks which the alert engineer had seen. The hour's delay to clear the tracks meant that as the train resumed its journey to Cincinnati the sky was beginning to lighten with the approaching dawn. Now the rope left dangling from the wall could be seen any time, if indeed it had not already been spotted. If a telegraph message had reached the Cincinnati station, authorities probably would be swarming onto the train. As they approached the Cincinnati suburbs, Morgan pulled the bell cord, signalling the engineer to stop the train. Paying no attention to the signal, the engineer rushed the train on toward Cincinnati. Thinking quickly with cool, calculating minds, Morgan moved to one platform, and Hines to another: then with all their strength they tightened the brakes on two of the cars. As the train slowed, first Hines, and then Morgan jumped. They landed next to a small campfire. Standing around the campfire warming themselves on this frosty morning of November 28th were two northern soldiers.

Chapter Eight

"Escape!"

Some thirty minutes before Morgan and Hines leaped from the train at about 6:30 a.m., the dawn of a new day began to lighten the sky over the prison back in Columbus. The dangling rope they had been unable to shake free from its anchor at the top of the wall hung in stark evidence of the success achieved by men desperate to be free. "ESCAPE!" screamed the guard as he burst into Warden Merion's office. Guards swarmed through the prison. Immediately they checked General Morgan's cell on the second tier. It was occupied. At least Morgan had not escaped, but seven of Morgan's officers were missing.

Merion immediately did what he knew he had to do. He sent a report to the new Federal commanding officer at Camp Chase who had replaced General Mason the previous day:

> SEVEN REBEL PRISONERS ES-
> CAPED FROM HERE LAST NIGHT. THEY
> WERE REPORTED LOCKED UP BY SER-
> GEANT MOON, BUT WERE NOT IN
> THEIR CELLS AT THE TIME. THEY
> UNDOUBTEDLY HID OUT IN THE YARD
> AND SCALED THE WALL WITH ROPE
> LADDERS. THERE HAS BEEN BRIBERY
> SOMEWHERE.

After the initial prisoner count, followed by the report sent to the Federal Commander, Merion's guards began a cell-by-cell check of the prisoners. Only then, nearly an hour after the initial discovery of the escape, did they realize that the prisoner in John Morgan's cell was *not* the infamous General, but rather his brother Richard. Merion was beside himself with anger and frustration. *General Morgan had escaped after all!*

Seven cells on Range One were locked, but no one was inside - only dummies made of old uniforms and bed clothes. Still they thought Sgt. Moon had been bribed to lock empty cells. He would likely hang for it. But then they opened Cell No. 20 — Hines' cell — and on his pillow was the note he had left as he had disappeared through his escape hole into the tunnel below:

> Castle Merion Cell No. 20
> Nov. 27, 1863
> Commencement - Nov. 4, 1863
> Conclusion - Nov. 20th, 1863
> No. of hours for labor per day - 3
> Tools - two small knives

Because Hines knew Merion couldn't understand French, in order to taunt him further, he added:

> *La patience est amére, mais son fruit est doux.*
>
> Th. H. Hines
>
> Capt. C.S.A

Merion didn't take time to worry about the translation: "By order of my six honorable Confederates"; he was boiling with anger and frustration. How could they have escaped? Merion next did what he knew he had to do, no matter how loathe he was to do it. Ohio Governor David Todd had to know about the situation as soon as possible, and it was up to Merion to tell him. Still placing the blame on Sgt. Moon, rather than on either himself or General Mason, he sent a telegram to Governor Todd advising him of Morgan's and six of his officers' escape, and blamed the success of his escape on a guard, whom he claimed had been bribed. Within minutes an ominous telegram left the governor's office destined for Secretary of War Stanton's office in Washington:

> I REGRET TO ANNOUNCE THE ESCAPE OF JOHN MORGAN AND FIVE OTHERS [there were *six* others] FROM THE PENITENTIARY LAST NIGHT. THEY DUG OUT UNDER THE WALLS, I CANNOT CHARGE ANYONE IN THE MILITARY SERVICE WITH NEGLIGENCE. THE WARDEN AND HIS GUARD ARE ALONE TO BLAME. SHALL TAKE ALL MEASURES TO RECAPTURE HIM. HAVE INSTRUCTED THE COMMANDER OF THIS PLACE TO OFFER A REWARD OF $1,000 WHICH I HOPE YOU WILL APPROVE.

Without waiting for a reply from Washington, Todd had $1,000 reward posters printed and circulated. The number of escapees on the posters was wrong, Hines' name was misspelled, and by the time Todd got word that, with Lincoln's approval, the amount of the reward had been upped to $5,000 by Stanton, the ink on the posters was already dry.

Governor Todd ordered his own immediate investigation, and guards, soldiers, officials, and newspaper reporters all swarmed through the cellblock. The evening edition of the Columbus *Dispatch* told exactly what the reporter had

Edwin McMasters Stanton, Lincoln's Secretary of War. Stanton received the telegram in his Washington office from Ohio Governor Todd advising of Morgan's escape. Stanton upped the reward for Morgan's recapture from $1,000 to $5,000 after conferring with Lincoln.

seen: holes in the cement floors of the cells, the tunnel dug below the cells, and the opening from the tunnel into the prison yard. The braided rope, still dangling from the top of the outer wall, told the rest of the story. The reporter concluded his story with the following remarks: "Energetic means are in operation to ferret out the mystery which appears to hang over their escape, and a few days only will elapse until evidence will appear, if any, of the knowledge of the collusion of outsiders with the manner or means of their escape."

Every home, attic, stable, and outhouse in Columbus was searched. Someone finally thought about the railroad, and a telegram was dispatched to train conductor Eckert, who was asleep in the Burnet House in Cincinnati. Morgan and six of his captains had escaped, he was told. Had he seen any suspicious men on his train? He immediately realized that the two men he had taken to be drovers were, in fact, Morgan and one of his captains. He wired this information back to Columbus, but by that time Morgan and Hines were already in Kentucky.

"What in thunder did you jump off that train for?" one of the two soldiers around the campfire by the railroad tracks asked Morgan. He quickly replied, "What's the use of a man going on into town when he lives out here? Besides, what's it to you?" he added. "Nothing, I guess," the soldier answered, as Morgan and Hines moved on toward the nearby Ohio River, which paralleled the tracks.

At the river's edge, they came upon a boy with a skiff. "What will you take to row us across the river?" Morgan asked the lad. For two dollars, they were soon on the opposite shore in Newport, Kentucky.

Chapter Nine

Into
Mattie's Arms

Although Kentucky claimed neutrality during the war, Kentuckians' sympathy was divided pretty evenly between the South and the North. Fortunately for Morgan and Hines, the first house they reached belonged to a known Rebel sympathizer. Morgan had a servant carry a note upstairs announcing who he was. Promptly a guide was sent to him who led them to Dr. William Robinson Thomas' home, which was four miles south of the river in Boone County.

In the physician's home, they sat down to breakfast, their first meal since dinner the previous evening in the prison dining room. As they ate, the doctor's two daughters hovered over them, excited that the great general who had escaped from prison was right there in their home. One of the girls noticed that his hands were red and raw. Morgan explained that their rope had burned his hands when he slid down it to get over the prison wall. The girls giggled and could hardly contain their excitement at the thoughts of such a daring adventure. The older girl asked for a lock of his hair, which Morgan permitted her to cut. He remarked that she was a better barber than the last one he had had, because he was the jailer who had cut off all his hair and had shaved his beard.

Dr. Thomas gave horses to Morgan and Hines to speed them on their way, and his twelve-year-old son proudly guided them on to the home of Henry Corwin in Union

County. Evening had came by the time they reached the Corwin home, which meant they had not had any sleep for two days. Exhausted, they fell into bed and slept until Sunday afternoon. A devoted Confederate, Corwin, too old to go to war, gave them money and fresh horses, and his young son guided them further south through Boone County, then through Gallatin County, and on into Owen County. The Corwin lad was not familiar with the countryside beyond that area, so they sent him back home and continued on alone, posing as drovers.

It was now the first of December, and the day was cold. They had pushed on all day and into the night. By two a.m., cold and hungry, they resolved to take their chances and approach the next farmhouse. The house was isolated, far from any town. Boldly, they rapped on the door. The owner, Pollard, answered himself and let them in. They had decided to pose as hog dealers who had taken a wrong turn and become lost. As Morgan was explaining their predicament to the sleepy Pollard, Hines noticed a copy of *The Cincinnati Enquirer* lying on the table. The newspaper's headlines proclaimed that Morgan and six of his officers had escaped from the Ohio Penitentiary. Since the *Enquirer* was a Democratic paper, Hines reasoned that Pollard was pro-southern. Trying to sound casual, Hines remarked, "I see that Morgan, Hines, and five officers have escaped." "Yes," Pollard replied, "and you are Captain Hines, are you not?" Hines bowed low and turned to his traveling companion. "Permit me to introduce General Morgan."

Back at the Ohio Penitentiary, Warden Merion was determined to prove bribery and collusion in order to shift the blame away from himself. He assigned E.N. Desellen of his prison staff to investigate and make a detailed report on every facet of the escape. Desellen set about his task in the manner of a detective sifting clues. "The appearance," his report began, "indicates that the noiseless push of a foot broke down the cement flooring at the proper time and opened a free passageway."

He examined the tunnel and found "an irregular arched hole thirty inches high and in one place five feet wide cut through the foundation wall on which the air chamber rests. A right-angle hole eighteen inches by thirty has been carried forward and downward for about five feet. The tunnel is thirty inches wide at this point, and continues horizontally at the same width to the wall of the cell house." He deduced that the escaping men had scraped out more of the bottom of the passage in order to remove the lowest stone in the wall, for the depression had filled with water.

His report continued: "earth from the tunnel and stones from the wall have been passed back into the air chamber, forming an irregular heap about twenty-four feet long and sixteen inches deep." He also found several table knives which had obviously been used for digging, three crudely fashioned candleholders, a small wooden box and two wooden washbowls, which had likely been used to carry earth from the tunnel to the air chamber.

Desellen was simply unable to produce the kind of evidence Merion wanted. He could not tie any bribery or collusion into the picture. It appeared that the prisoners had simply tunneled their way to freedom. Meanwhile, Governor Todd's own investigation was still in progress, which resulted in the conclusion that "the escape could not have occurred had there been daily or even weekly inspections of the cells." General Mason's snap decision on November second, to let the rebels clean their own cells, now came back to haunt him. Mason was tracked down at his home in

Steubenville, Ohio, where he was spending a furlough. In order to get him away from the heat of the investigation, he was spirited away to San Francisco, where he assumed the command of a remote garrison. One of Mason's officers in charge of the guard detail at the prison, Lt. Judkins, assumed the blame and was summarily given a dishonorable discharge from the Union army.

After reviewing the results of four separate investigations, including the one commissioned by himself, Governor Todd wrote, "I am glad to know that there is not the slightest evidence to be found of fraud or corruption on the part of the officers, either civil or military, nor on the part of any individual citizen without or within the prison."

Farmer Polland, after guessing Morgan and Hines' identities, made them welcome to his home, let them sleep late the next morning, and sent them on their way with gifts of cattle whips in order to help them justify their covers as drovers and cattle buyers. They crossed the Cumberland River near Burkesville, where their now famous raid had begun back in early July. Pushing further south, they came to the Tennessee River, where they were joined by five other Rebel soldiers, and as they continued into Tennessee, they were attacked by Federal soldiers on horseback.

Hines, always ready in an instant with a deceptive tactic, shouted, "Hurry up, Major, or the Rebels will escape!" Hines proceeded to gallop away from Morgan and the others. The Union soldiers, with Hines in the lead, raced for several miles to catch Confederate soldiers who did not exist. However, the Yankee major finally noticed that there were no tracks in the soft earth - tracks Rebels would have made were they indeed being pursued. Smelling a rat, he called a halt, drew his pistol, and aimed it at Hines' head.

Livid with rage that he had been made a fool of, he demanded to know the name of his captive. "Captain Thomas H. Hines, Confederate States of America," was the terse reply. "General Morgan is by now some miles away," he added. Hines had once again, this time on the spur of the moment, engineered an escape for General John Hunt Morgan. But it was at the cost of his own hard-won freedom, which he was willing to sacrifice so that his leader could get away.

Morgan rode as hard and as far as he could. South through eastern Tennessee he traveled, through the snowy passes of the Smoky Mountains, and across the North Carolina border into the small town of Franklin. The next day he crossed North Carolina into Columbia, South Carolina, where he wired Mattie in Danville: JUST ARRIVED. WILL MAKE NO STOP UNTIL I REACH YOU.

It was Christmas eve, and Mattie, at home in Danville, Virginia, just across the North Carolina border, knew that her husband might arrive that night. She could not retire for excitement and sat up all night in her room waiting in anticipation for the moment she had dreamed of and prayed for over most of the past year. After midnight - it was now Christmas - she heard the knock at the front door. A servant answered and led John up to Mattie's room. She fell into his arms. Feeling her body next to his, he knew that she was no longer with child. He looked down at her inquisitively. She knew what his eyes were asking. "Oh, John, she broke into sobs — "she was *so beautiful.*"

The night John Morgan had made the most dramatic and incredible prison escape of the Civil War, his daughter had not only been born, she had died while he was on the train to Cincinnati.

Morgan and Mattie together after his dramatic escape from the Ohio State Penitentiary. Mattie again became pregnant, but Morgan did not live to see his second daughter, whom Mattie named "Johnnie" after him.

Chapter Ten
Epilogue
To Part One

Captains Sheldon and Taylor made it as far as Louis-ville, Kentucky, where they were recognized, arrested, and returned to the Ohio Penitentiary. They were locked into cells on Range Three (the *third* tier), and were treated more harshly than ever. Warden Merion, who was able to retain his position in spite of his proven negligence, made sure their cells were inspected daily.

Captain Magee made it back to his home in West Virginia, and as far as is known, remained there. Captains Bennett and Hockersmith fled together and eluded capture. In a bizarre turn of events, in later years, Hockersmith ran against Hines for the same political office - a judgeship in Kentucky. Hines won.

Hines, who duped the Yankee Major so that Morgan could get away, became the Major's prisoner, but he had little trouble in escaping that same night. He was confined in a log hut guarded by a single Union soldier. Hines was not called "wiley" without a reason. First he got the soldier laughing at his jokes and mimicry until tears ran down the soldier's face, and he doubled up with laughter. At that moment, Hines applied his knee to the guard's stomach as hard as he could, bolted out the door, mounted the soldier's horse, and rode off into the night. Chalk up still another escape for the sly Hines.

Courtesy, Mrs. John J. Winn

After his escape, Hines had this picture taken for his fiancée, Nancy Sproule. He was 26 years of age.

He made his way to Richmond, Virginia, the Confederate capital, where he was ordered by Confederate President Jefferson Davis to Toronto to organize a subversive movement among the Canadians. When that plan failed, Hines endeavored to foment a revolution in Chicago and very nearly succeeded. However, a former Confederate officer, Lt. James Shanks, turned informant, infiltrated Hines' underground army, and disclosed the location of the Chicago hideout to Union forces. "A blacker-hearted villain never lived," Hines was later to write of the Confederate traitor Shanks.

With Shanks' disclosure, 3,000 Union troops descended on Chicago and captured all of Hines' men, except, of course, Hines himself. The cache of weapons confiscated in Hines' arsenal included 210 double-barreled shotguns, 350 Colt revolvers, 100 Henry rifles, 13,000 rounds of ammunition, and assorted knives and lances. They weren't playing games; they obviously meant business. Chicago was panicked. A dragnet for Hines, with a house-to-house search, was begun. Could Hines possibly escape again?

Of course he could! And this, his last escape, was probably the most bizarre of them all. Hines sought refuge in the Chicago home of Dr. Edward W. Edwards, a Confederate sympathizer and the leader of the Sons of Liberty. On November 7, 1864, at 10:30 p.m., Hines fell asleep in Edwards' home with a dagger under his pillow. At 11:30 a.m., Edwards awakened him advising that a Union patrol was in front of the house preparing to enter and search. It is difficult to believe what the conniving Hines did next.

It so happened that Dr. Edwards' wife was deathly ill with diphtheria, a highly contagious and often fatal disease. She tossed and turned with a burning fever. Over the protest of her husband, Hines actually climbed into bed with the gravely ill and contagious Mrs. Edward. With his dagger he cut a large slit in the box-like mattress she was lying on, inserted himself down into the mattress *underneath* of the dying woman, and remained perfectly still. The Union soldiers searched the house, but they failed to look underneath Mrs. Edwards.

The next day Hines slipped out of Chicago unnoticed. He never did develop diphtheria. Whether or not Mrs. Edwards survived is unknown.

After the war ended in 1865, Hines married his long-time sweetheart and fiancée, Nancy Sproule. He became the editor of the Memphis, Tennessee, *Daily Appeal*. He later was admitted to the Kentucky bar and not only practiced law, but went on to serve two terms as Chief Justice of Kentucky's Court of Appeals. In 1898 his wife, Nancy, died suddenly. Hines was crushed and could not be consoled. He followed her in death within three weeks. Considered by many to be "the most dangerous man in the Confederacy", Captain Thomas H. Hines died of a broken heart.

Meanwhile, John Hunt Morgan was up to his old tricks. Issuing the following notice, he organized a new group of raiders and staged another grandiose raid through Kentucky in 1864. Although the Confederate cause looked bleak, Morgan never stopped trying.

"Soldiers!

I am once more among you, after a long and painful imprisonment. I am anxious to be again in the field. I, therefore, call on soldiers of my command to assemble at the place of rendezvous. ... Your country needs your service; the field of operation is wide, and the future glorious, if we only deserve it. Remember how many of your true comrades are still pining in a a felon's cell. They call loudly on you for help. They expect it. Will you disappoint them? The work before us will be arduous, and will require brave hearts and willing hands. Let no man falter or delay."

John H. Morgan
Brigadier General, C.S.A.

The new raid finally led to Greeneville in Eastern Tennessee, and with the Federals on his trail, in hot pursuit as usual, he spent the night of September 3, 1864, in the Williams mansion in the center of town. He thought he was far enough ahead of the enemy to get a good night's sleep before he pushed on in the morning.

But as he slept, the enemy caught up, and learning his whereabouts, they surrounded the house. Had Hines been there, perhaps he could have pulled another trick out of his bag. But Morgan was on his own, and his luck had just run out. He tried to escape through the garden in the back of the house. As he tried to slip through the shrubbery, a girl watching from across the street called out, "That's him!" That's Morgan over there among the grape vines."

Morgan shouted, "Don't shoot! I surrender." Private Andrew J. Campbell of Company G, Thirteenth Tennessee Cavalry was closest to Morgan. "Surrender and be damned. I know you," Campbell shouted back as he pulled the trigger. As Morgan slumped to the ground, Campbell muttered, "I've killed the damned horse thief." Morgan died instantly, just as his young brother Tom had died a year earlier, with a bullet from a Union rifle through his heart.

Williams home where Morgan was killed. This picture was made shortly after the war.

Pvt. Andrew J. Campbell, Morgan's assassin. After he killed Morgan, he was promoted to Sergeant.

Mattie, who again became pregnant before her huband's death, had another daughter. She named her Johnnie Hunt Morgan after her father, who was never to see either of his daughters. Both Mattie and Johnnie died in 1888, Johnnie of typhoid fever at age 23, just two months after her marriage to a Presbyterian minister; and Mattie at age 47.

Among Mattie's personal effects found after her death was the last letter she had received from John Morgan before his escape. It was dated November 2, 1863. Inside the envelope, still pressed into the letter, were the violets he had sent her from prison.

Brigadier General John Hunt Morgan in 1864. His last known portrait. Col. Basil Duke, after his release from the Ohio Penitentiary, was shocked at his brother-in-law, Morgan's appearance. Morgan had become depressed about the outcome of the war, which was reflected in his countenance.

Morgan family burial plot at Lexington, Kentucky.

Introduction
To Part Two

The details of the prison escape as recounted in Part One represent the well-authenticated and documented story as is generally accepted by historians and Morgan scholars. The facts are clearly set forth in the definitive work on Morgan's raid, the 595 page *A History of Morgan's Calvary* by his brother-in-law and second-in-command, Basil W. Duke, originally published in 1867. Yet, details of the escape plan have been challenged by one of the other six escapees!

During January 1994 I was invited to speak to the New Albany (Indiana) Rotary Club on the subject of the Battle of Corydon. During that battle, on July 9, 1863, Morgan and his raiders captured Indiana's first state capital. I concluded my talk by mentioning Morgan's exploits after he moved on from Corydon, including his capture and escape from prison.

After the program, a Rotarian, Roger Reynolds, D.D.S., came to me and explained that he was directly descended from Capt. Hockersmith, and that he was in possession of the "Hockersmith papers" written by his great-great grandfather more than a century ago. He added that the Hockersmith account of the escape differed from the generally accepted version. Would I like to study the papers?

Of course I asked to see them, and when I read them I was flabbergasted. It was obvious that Captains Hockersmith and Hines had no love for each other, and in a bizarre twist of fate, in 1875, twelve years after the escape, they opposed one another in a political campaign for a judgeship with Kentucky's Court of Appeals.

As part of his campaign stategy, Hockersmith accused Hines of taking credit for masterminding and implementing the celebrated escape, when it was actually he, Hockersmith, who was the brains and driving force behind it. But apparently the public did not buy Hockersmith's story, as he lost the election to Hines, who become the Chief Justice.

It would be easy to dismiss Hockersmith's claims as mere political chicanery but for the fact that the story as written and recorded by him seems to ring with an aura of sincerity and authenticity. Could it be that Hines' ego led him to assume credit for planning the escape that was actually masterminded by Hockersmith?

It doesn't seem likely. Yet, as stated, Hockersmith's first person account of the escape is difficult to dismiss because of its seeming sincerity from a man of sterling character. His 1915 obituary in the *Confederate Veteran* stated, "Captain Hockersmith was not only a brave soldier, but it is perhaps as a citizen that his life shines out best. He had been a devoted member of the Methodist Church for more that sixty years, and was a Mason and a Shriner. No man who ever lived in Madisonville was more genuinely loved and respected by all."

Which account is the more accurate - Hines' or Hockersmith's – we will never really know. Obviously one or the other has shaded the facts to his own advantage. Part Two presents, in his own words, Capt. Hockersmith's version of the escape. As to which of the accounts is indeed correct, you, the reader, must decide for yourself.

W. Fred Conway - April 1994

92

PART TWO

MORGAN'S ESCAPE

*A Thrilling Story
Of War Times*

*A True History Of The Raid
Of General Morgan And His Men
Through Kentucky, Indiana And Ohio;
Their Incarceration In
The Columbus Penitentary,
Escape Therefrom And
Tragic Death Of The Intrepid Leader*

BY: CAPT.L.D. HOCKERSMITH

How General Morgan and His Men Managed to Get Out of the Penitentary.

By Capt. L. D. Hockersmith.

There are those who will remember that about 18 years ago, [in 1885] I wrote a series of articles for *The Gleaner*, a paper then published at Madisonville, which paper was edited by C. C. Givens, now of *The Hustler* and J. J. Glenn, now editor of *The Graphic*. These articles were an account of the Escape of Morgan and his men from the Columbus, Ohio, Penitentiary, which escape occured on the 29th day of November 1863. The editor of *The Graphic* has asked permission to reproduce the series of articles published in *The Gleaner* in 1885. The editor of the *The Graphic* wishes to say a few things in this connection as an explanation in reference to the re-publication of the next few chapters of the escape of General Morgan and his men from the Columbus penitentiary on the night of the 28th; or the early morning of the 29th of November 1863. The following accounts were written by Captain Hockersmith 18 years ago next summer and were published in the *Hopkins County Gleaner*, of which paper we were one of the editors.

The articles were called forth on account of a number of different reports that had been published by others in which the facts connected with that escape were not given just as they had occured. Captain Hockersmith planned, and by the aid of others, executed the escape from that prison. Of this there is no earthly doubt. These articles were written nearly eighteen years ago, and Capt. Hockersmith does not now wish to change a single statement he made at that time.

At the time of the publication of these articles, we then wrote and published in *The Gleaner*, the following editorial:

MORGAN'S ESCAPE

"In another column will be found the first of the series of articles from the pen of Capt L. D. Hockersmith, in which he proposes to give his version of the escape of General Morgan and his men from the State prison at Columbus, Ohio, on the night of the 28th of November, 1863. It is now nearly twenty-two years since these brave men, who were prisoners of war, made that most wonderful escape, an escape that for engenuity, bravery, and thought is equaled in history only by that of Baron Trenck. At the time of that occurrence, the newspapers of the Union were full of various accounts of how that escape was made. During the struggle of the two contending armies of the United States, the various war correspondents who visited the prison made different reports as to how Gen. Morgan and his men managed to elude the vigilance of those under whose charge they were placed. Not until after the war had closed could those in position to know, have an opportunity to write a true history of that memorable event.

Capt. Thos. H. Hines has on different occasions given a history of this affair, and at all times has made himself the hero of the tale. Seven years ago he rode into office by this means, and when asked by the man who had been the chief instrument in securing the freedom of this office-seeker, to do justice in the case, he promised to set the matter right. Did he do it? By no means. Today he is again a candidate for the same position, and throws to the world a new history of the stirring times of '63; again makes himself the noble hero of the wonderful escape, ignoring or misrepresenting those whose brain and nerve opened the prison bars of the penitentiary for himself and others. Capt. Hockersmith is a citizen of the town of Madisonville and was born in Lawrenceburg.

This has been his home since 1855, except the time he served in the "Lost Cause" as Captain of Co. C., 10th Kentucky Cavalry. We wish to say for the benefit of those who may not know Capt. Hockersmith, that the State of Kentucky does not contain within her limits a nobler, truer or braver man than he, and that each and every statement that he makes is true to the letter. He is not writing these articles for gain or for office, but in the interest of truth and justice. It is not his desire or intention to wrong any man in this, but simply to see that there is a true account published of the events that are now being used to again place a man in position who seeks to obtain it at the expense of others."

This story will deal with the prison life of General Morgan and his men, of the plans they laid, of the execution of the work and the escape from the penitentiary of that early November morning, as told by Capt. Hockersmith nearly 18 years ago. Capt. Hockersmith says:

Gentlemen;— I have recently had the privilege of reading several accounts of the escape of General Morgan and six others from the penitentiary at Columbus, Ohio, on the night of the 28th November, 1863. These accounts to me have been both pleasant and painful; pleasant, that they call to mind the scenes of by-gone days, and the many stirring events connected with that memorable struggle; painful, because in all the published reports of that escape from the old State prison, not one of them so far has been correct. Had the brave Gen. Morgan lived to give his version of that affair it would not be necessary at this time for me to say anything about it. He would have seen that every man connected therewith should have had justice done him, and that the honors if any there were, in the escape, should rest where they justly belong, and not upon one whose only work was to sit in his cell door and study French. In every published account heretofore, Capt. Hines has made himself the hero of the whole escape, while others have been made to occupy inferior positions, or have been entirely ignored.

The *Southern Bivouac* for June has a lengthy article upon the escape of Morgan and his men, written by this hero Hines, and vouched for by Gen. Basil W. Duke, who seems to be grooming the Judge for the coming Appellate election. I am much surprised at many statements that he has made to the world in that article of his. He claims the honor of originating the scheme to escape, and also to have laid out and carried into effect the plans, the successful workings of which enabled us to once more breathe the air of liberty. I propose, through an humble citizen of this Commonwealth, by the consent of the editors of *The Gleaner*, through their most excellent paper, to give a true version of the affair, let it hurt whom it may. Gross injustice has been done to many good men, brave and true, in the accounts heretofore published of this marvelous escape, while some have reaped honor therefrom who were not entitled to it.

I say positively that Judge Hines did not originate the idea of escape. Capt. Sam Taylor and myself had the plans all laid and ready to begin work before he, Hines, knew anything whatever of the affair. On the last day of October, 1863, Capt. Hines came into cell No. 28, which was the one occupied by myself. Capt. Taylor and I were seated on my bed engaged in conversation in regard to our escape, when Hines came in and asked if we "were not plotting against the whites." Capt. Taylor replied: "You are damned mighty right," which was his way of swearing.

Capt. Hines certainly cannot forget that then and there we informed him of our intentions, and on certain conditions let him into the secret as a third party. At the proper time I shall let the reader know what these conditions were, and shall also probably ask the Capt. some questions that will surprise the many. The truth must and shall be told, let it effect whom it may. In Basil W. Duke's History he gets my name as James Hockersmith. James Hockersmith was a younger brother of mine who was in the Federal army. I know not where Gen. Duke got his information, unless it was from Capt. Hines, who has written several articles for the press of the country in which he claims to have originated the plans of the escape. General Duke, himself, though a prisoner was in no way connected with either the plans or the execution of that memorable event.

In Collins' History of Kentucky there is another account given by Judge Hines, which is far from being correct, and in which he again figures as the hero. Several years ago, while the captain was a candidate for Judge of the Court of Appeals, he came to Madisonville, my home, where he was almost a stranger. He sent for me to call upon him, and seemed surprised to find that I was opposed to him in his race. I gave as my reason that in his account in Collins' History that I and others had been ignored, while he had taken to himself the whole credit for the escape.

He said that I judged him wrong; that he had referred Collins to Capt. Sheldon and myself for a correct account of this, and that the history was to be revised and that he himself would see that justice was done to all. He failed to do this, but is now writing a history himself, backed by Basil Duke, and that history is farther from being correct than the first.

I propose to correct some of the many errors that have been written in regard to that midnight escape and hope that neither Judge Hines nor any one will take offense at what may be said or written in this series of articles, as it is my desire to simply give a true version of the whole affair, to neither rob any one of any honor due him, nor give to any man credit that belongs to another.

Now I ask, is it reasonable to suppose that Hines would select three members of the 10th Kentucky, Capts. Sam Taylor, Jake Bennett and L. D. Hockersmith, entire strangers to him, until they had met in prison, to carry out his plans and designs, in preference to members of his own command?

Let us now suppose a case, so that we may be able to see who could properly describe the scenes of that November of 1863. Two men go through the Mammoth Cave, one of them rushing through as if for life itself. His time is limited; if he fails to get through in a certain time he forfeits liberty and perhaps life itself. The other has days and weeks before him; he takes his time; he lives in there; which of the two can give the better description of this cavern? It is the same with this air chamber under the penitentiary. For twenty-eight days myself and others were underground, digging and working with such tools as we could secure, while the only time Capt. Hines was underground was on that night as we all passed out hurriedly through the hole made by hands other than his own. The Captain on that occasion, I can assure you, did not stop in the air chamber to make any examination, but pulled through as rapidly as possible.

I propose in the next article to give a plan of the cells occupied by each one of the prisoners of war, and as far as possible a description of the penitentiary in which we were confined. I shall, in the future, give the conversation, suggestions and workings of these men seeking for the liberty of freedom, and shall go into minute details of everything connected with this memorable escape, with the progress of each day's work from the 27th of October until 7:30 A. M. on November 29th, 1863, when just before Gen. Morgan jumped from the platform of the moving train in the suburbs of Cincinnati, he embraced Capt. Bennett and myself, and said: "Boys, Goodbye, farewell! farewell!" It was a final farewell; we never met again.

PLAN OF PRISON

Cols. D. Morgan and W. W. Ward's regiments were captured July 19th, 1863, at Buffington's Island, Ohio. Cols. B. W. Duke and — Smith's commands were captured July 20, Lieu't. Col. Coleman and command were captured July 20, at Cheshire, Ohio; Gen. Morgan and the remainder of his command were captured July 26, and taken at once to the Ohio State prison, as I was informed, while we, the first that were captured, were carried to Cincinnati, confined in the city lockup about 48 hours; taken from there to Johnson's Island, where we remained four days, and then were removed to the State penitentiary at Columbus, Ohio. The following is the plan of the cells in the prison and the disposition of the prisoners:

CELL PLAN OF PRISON

4	4	4	
			2
9 Magee	35		
	34	3	
	33		
	32		2
	31		
	30		
Bennett	29		
Hockersmith	28		
	27		
9	26	3	
	25		2
	24		
	23		
	22		
Col. D. Morgan	21		
Hines	20		
	19		
Sheldon	18		2
9	17	3	
	16		
S. Taylor	15		
	14		
	13		
	12		
	11		
	10	8	6
	9		5
	8		
9	7		
	6		
	5		
	4		
	3		
	2		
9	1	7 1 7	2

EXPLANATION

1—Entrance to hall in front of cells.

2—Outside wall of main building.

3—Hall in front of cells.

4—South side of cells in first range and east wing of prison.

5—Stove flue.

6—Ventilation in flue.

7—Sentinels.

8—Stove

Partition wall between convicts and prisoners of war.

These cells were 3 feet 6 inches wide, about 7 feet long and about 7 feet high, with a heavy iron grate door to each, with spring locks and were in tiers or ranges. The diagram shows Range No. 1, while Range No. 2 was immediately above. On the left were the cells in which the convicts were confined. The floors were arched with three arches of brick, while the top was made of sand cement called concrete, making the floor about 2 1/2 feet thick. In addition to this there was in each cell a broad plank in front of the bed 15 inches wide and five feet long. This plank was to keep the feet off the damp concrete floor. The bed-stead was a small skeleton, hung to the partition wall by small iron hinges, so that it could be turned back against the wall to allow the prisoner room for a small promenade; there was also a small three-legged stool to each cell, and a strip of plank 1 inch thick, 3 inches wide and 3 feet long which was used as a prop to the bed. This completed the furniture.

The following was the disposition of the prisoners in the cells, with the number and range:

PRISONERS OF FIRST RANGE

Name of prisoner	No. of Cell
Col. W. W. Ward,	1
Capt. P. H. Tharp,	2
Capt. J. L. Jones,	3
Capt. Thos. W. Bullit,	4
Capt. A. Thomas,	5
Lt. Col. J. T. Tucker,	7
Capt E. T. Rochester,	8
Capt. Thos. H. Shanks,	9
Capt . R. E . Roberts,	10
Capt. L. W. Trafton,	14
Capt. Sam B. Taylor,	15
Capt . R . D . Logan,	16
Lieut. Tom Mourland,	17
Capt. R. Sheldon,	18
Capt. E. W. McLean,	19
Capt. Thos. Henry Hines,	20
Col. R. C. Morgan,	21
T. E. Earton, Lt. Master,	22
Capt. G. C. Mullins,	23
Capt. J. L. N Dickens,	24
Capt. M. S. Edwards,	25
Capt. M. Griffin,	26
Capt. L. D. Holloway,	27
Capt. L. D. Hockersmith,	28
Capt. J. C. Bennett,	29
Maj. J. B. McCreary,	30
Col. D. Howard Smith,	31
Capt. James N. Taylor,	32
Capt. B. S. Barton,	32
Capt. H. C. Ellis,	33
Capt. J. B. Hunter,	34
Capt. J. S. Magee,	35

SECOND RANGE

Name of prisoner	No. of Cell
Col. R. S. Cluke,	1
Capt. T. M. Coombs,	2
Capt. J. H. Hamby,	3
Capt. C. C. Morgan,	4
Capt . E . F . Cheatham,	5
Maj. H. A. Higby,	6
Capt. Hall Gibson,	7
Major W. G. Owen,	8
Capt. D. R. Williams,	9
Capt. E. D. Warder,	10
Capt. S. Morgan,	11
Lieut. J. H. Croston,	12
Capt. Buford A. Lacy,	13
Capt. T. R. Boyd,	14
Wash C. Shame, Aid-de-Camp,	16
Capt. E. S. Dawson,	17
Capt. J. S. Ambrose,	18
Lt. Col. C. Coleman,	20
Capt. W. R. Cunningham,	21
Capt. Isaac Baker,	22
Capt. G. M. Coleman,	24
Capt. C. L. Bennett,	25
Major R. S. Bullock,	26
Basil W. Duke,	27
Capt. A. S. Brunner,	28
Capt. J. S. Chapman,	29
Capt Jas W. Mitchell,	29
Capt. M. D. Logan,	30
Capt. C. H. Morgan,	31
Maj. W. G. Bullit,	32
Jos B. Cole, Inspecting Gen.,	33
Maj. W. P. Elliott,	34
Gen. John H. Morgan,	35

OHIO PENITENTIARY

Maj. Thos Steel in Hospital.

Capt. C. C. Campbell sick in Hospital.

Capt. John H. Woolf sick in Hospital.

The main outside wall which inclosed this hall as well as the cells, was some taller than the cell building. The cells are five tiers or ranges high. The floor of this hall was stone and laid in solid earth with no ventilation under it. This outside wall had no connection with the cell walls whatever, with the exception of the ground floor. I have been thus particular in giving the names of parties, with their cells and locations, as I shall frequently in after communications have need to refer to many of them. We wish the reader to study well the various positions laid down in this article, with the names of the parties connected therewith. In my next chapter I shall commence with the plans suggested and adopted for our escape.

In the last chapter, in describing the cell floors, I omitted to explain a fill of 8 or 10 inches, made of spawls of rock, from the size of a grain of sand up to six inches or more in size. These spawls are pieces or chips which fly from rock or brick in dressing them when getting them ready for use. The object of this filling was to give a level base for the 6 inches of concrete which formed the floor of the cells.

The entire building was covered with a metal roof, through which there are several skylights. About the middle of the outer main wall there was a down pipe or tin spout to convey the water from the roof to the ground, and which was fastened to the wall with iron cleats. Mr. — Scott, who was one of the wardens of the penitentiary, one day gave us the history of two convicts who had managed to make their escape by going through one of the skylights on the roof, and then by climbing down this pipe or spout to the ground. The revelation of this wonderful escape, I honestly believe, led to ours.

Up to this time I had scarcely entertained an idea or a thought that there was any chance for us to get out of the prison, except by being turned out through the door by which we had come in. But Scott's story set me to thinking that I could at least manage some means to regain my liberty. The architect, in laying out his designs for the erection of this prison in the Buck Eye State, intended no doubt to build a house from which no man should ever be able to escape.

But he failed, as all others had done before. It is said that man cannot build what man cannot pull down or destroy. Yet when one passes through one of these immense iron-grated doors as a prisoner, and the turn-key, with his lever, throws one of those 1 x 3 inch bolts into its socket, he leaves all hope behind.

JAKE BENNETT

When Capt. Jake Bennett was taken to his cell the guard gave him a shove as he ushered him in and said: "Go in there, you damned Reb, and let's see if you can get but out of there." The Capt. cast his eyes to the ceiling and exclaimed: "No, my God! I might as well try to get out of hell."

Jake Bennett was Captain of Co. A., 10th Kentucky Cavalry, and from some cause had been sent to Camp Chase, where the privates of Morgan's command were confined. While there he attempted to make his escape, but failed and was sent to Columbus for safe keeping. When I heard Capt. Bennett make his remark about the infernal regions, I at that time thought that he was correct. It was after this that I conceived the idea of regaining my liberty.

STUDYING ABOUT ESCAPE

On the 27th of October, 1863, I began looking around to see how and where there might be a possibility of getting away from under the surveillance of those Yankees who were watching us so closely. While walking through the hall-way I was impressed with the idea that I could crawl through the stove flue and thus get out on top of the prison. I soon caught an opportunity to examine the ventilator in the flue, which was located near the floor. I believed that there could be but one thing in the way to prevent a success, and that was the guards who was stationed so near the outlet. It seemed at first that it would be a difficult matter to get the ventilator from the place assigned to it by the architect. However, I ventured near enough that day to see that it could be removed without disturbing the wall. I did nothing more then, as it was getting late in the evening and not being long until our supper would be ready.

SHAM READING

That night while in bed I thought the matter over again and again, and the next morning a 9 o'clock a.m., the 28th, I was at my post with testament in hand, seated on the stone floor leaning against the wall, near enough to the ventilator to touch it with my right hand, and more eager, if possible, than the day before to accomplish my purposes. You may rest assured that my mind was more upon the undertaking than it was upon the testament I was reading. Four o'clock in the afternoon came and found me no nearer out than when I first began. Again I was locked in my cell for the night to dream of liberty. At six o'clock the next morning we were all turned out of our cells to prepare for breakfast, and, as the usual custom, marched in single file to the well or hydrant, where there was a large trough filled with water, where we performed our morning ablutions and then ate our morning meal.

THAT VENTILATOR

At 10 o'clock my opportunities were better than ever before. The guards seemed to be more careless than usual. I succeeded in getting the ventilator loose, and fully intended sometime during the day to take my departure from the hall, through the stove flue to the top of house, and about dusk to go down the pipe and forever shake the dust of Columbus from my feet. While I was rejoicing in my own mind at the thought of my early deliverance, Capt Sam Taylor, who had been watching my maneuvers, suspected me, approached me and in an undertone, to my surprise, said: "What in the hell have you been sitting at the hole all day for?" meaning the ventilator in the flue. I replied, "None of your business," all in good humor of course; for we were the very best of friends.

CAPT. SAM TAYLOR

We immediately walked to the rear of the hall. The Capt. took me by the arm and walked with me as far as cell No. 35. We then turned around and returned to cell No. 28 which we entered and sat down upon my bed. Capt Taylor had all the time been trying to find out what I had been planning. At first I gave him no satisfaction. He then appealed to me to tell him the truth, and asked me if I had not been planning an escape through that stove flue? I answered him that I was not only planning, but that I intended to make my exit through that same place, and requested him to keep silent upon the subject.

VENTILATOR PLANS ABANDONED

He insisted that I could not succeed, and gave several reasons for his belief. I did not agree with him, and gave him to understand that I could not afford to abandon my plans unless something better was offered. He then suggested that as I was a mechanic and brick mason that I could perhaps cut through these walls. That idea had never before presented itself to my mind; I had almost forgotten that I ever knew how to handle the trowel or to lay brick, but the idea was a good one and I liked it. Several suggestions were made and abandoned, as to how we should proceed. We then separated. By this time I had about abandoned the plan of going out through the flue.

LAYING PLANS

On October 30th, at 8 o'clock a.m., Capt. Taylor and myself got together in his cell, No. 15, and renewed the conversation of the evening before. We laid many plans and made many suggestions, none of which seemed to be feasible. I then proposed that we go through the floor and cut under the foundations. My knowledge and experience taught me that there must be a ventilation under the cell floors, otherwise it would be so damp that men could not live in them.

SOUNDS THE FLOOR

While thus reasoning, Taylor picked up the strip of plank used to prop up the bed and with the end knocked on the floor of the cell. It sounded hollow, and he then stepped out of the cell door and with the same plank knocked on the floor of the hall, which produced dull, dead sound. We were then satisfied that my suggestion was correct – that the ventilation was beneath the cells.

PLAN AGREED UPON

Then my plan to cut through the floor was at once agreed upon. We at that time knew nothing of the thickness of the floor, and there was no way of gaining the desired information but to go to work and cut through and find out. The difficulty now was to secure tools with which to begin work, as we had nothing but pocket knives and some other small tools, such as files and saws, which we were permitted to have to make rings and such like with.

I proposed to do the work, the cutting of the cement, while Capt. Taylor was to conceal the mortar or whatever rubbish might be taken out as the work progressed. His proposition was to take the rubbish out in his pockets, throw it in the stoves, in the spit-boxes, scatter it around in the saw dust on the dining room floor or put it in any or all places where it would not be discovered. Capt. Taylor and myself by this time pretty well understood the task before us, and were selfish enough to undertake the job by ourselves, as up to this time we had taken no one into our confidence.

We had, as we supposed, all our arrangements made, ready to begin work the next day. It was under-

111

stood that our work would have to be done by daylight, because we were locked up in our cells during the night, and there could be no communication with one another between the hours of 6 p.m. and 6 a.m.

On the morning of the 31st of October at 8 o'clock Capt. Taylor and myself were in my cell, No. 28, further discussing the subject which had been uppermost in our minds for sometime, when the question arose as to whose cell we should begin the work in; not that we were particular as to the cell, but how should we get together after the work should be completed. We were separated at night, and we knew that the escape must be made in the dark. If we cut through the floor in his cell I should be left; if in mine, then he would be left.

CAPT. HINES COMES IN

While we were thus planning and talking Capt. Thomas H. Hines walked up to the door of my cell and addressed himself to us by saying: "Are you fellows plotting against the whites?" or words to that effect. Capt. Taylor replied: "You are mighty damned right." It was not long until Capt. Hines was let into the secret, Capt. Taylor communicating the same to him. Capt. Hines endorsed the plan with delight. We also informed him of the difficulty we had just been considering. He proposed that the work should be commenced in his cell, agreeing to take upon himself the responsibility of detection. Then the question came up again in reference to getting to the cell when the work was done, when Capt. Hines proposed to have the doors open at the proper time by sawing the bolts or eating them off with aquafortis. We accepted his proposition which was the condition.

ACCEPTED HINES PROPOSITION

Capt. Taylor and myself having heard Capt. Hines' propositions, and, accepting them, we told him that we had been considering a plan for getting Gen. Morgan out with us. The difficulty that presented itself was to get him from his cell being No. 35, second range, just above that of Capt. McGee, No. 35, first range. Yet it was determined that we would take him with us if possible. We at length agreed to lay the matter before him and see what he thought of our plans.

CALL ON GEN. MORGAN

We three went to Gen. Morgan, Capt. Hines acting as spokesman, while Capt. Taylor and myself listened and occasionally threw in a word. He heard us through, questioned us closely and was much surprised at the audacity of the undertaking. I do not believe at the time that he had any great confidence in the success of the enterprise. We informed him that he was to have nothing to do with the work, but must keep himself in the back ground so as to keep down suspicion. We left the cell and it was proposed by Hines and Taylor to take Capt.'s McGee and Sheldon into our confidence, while I selected Capt. Jake Bennett. There being no objections to the three persons named, they were invited into Capt. Hines cell and informed of our plans, and all readily agreed to them. Capt. Sheldon made some good suggestions as to how we should begin work, and how we should get the tools to begin with. I regard him as being one of the most determined men of the six.

PLANS FOR ESCAPE

Capt. McGee was a mechanic, a carpenter by profession, and the right man in the right place. Capt. Bennett expressed himself as being ready to do anything that we might impose upon him. I being a bricklayer Capt. Taylor proposed that I should superintend the work, Capt. Hines was to act as guard or sentinel, while Capt Taylor should conceal the rubbish, which he had formerly agreed to do. Each man having been assigned to his work, we yet had some other things to look after. We were not well supplied with tools. We had but two pocket knives among us. Sheldon's proposition to get knives from the table of course was adopted, with the understanding that we were to take but one at a time, for fear they should be missed.

CONFIDENCE GAME

The next thing was to manage to get the confidence of the guards so as to keep down any suspicion they might have of our intentions. It was the custom of the wardens to sweep and inspect the cells, or cause it to be done by the convicts, at least once every day. The hall was looked after twice each day. They were particular in keeping a clean prison. We were not allowed to spit tobacco juice on the floor, neither were we allowed to throw apple or peach parings or seed, strips of paper or litter of any kind on the floor. So in order to prevent their sweeping our cells Capt. Hines proposed that we get brooms and do our own sweeping. We were allowed to furnish our cells with any kind of furniture or ornaments we chose to buy, and some of them were handsomely furnished, which helped to keep down or hide any suspicion that might arise from our proposed sweeping.

We were also forbidden to make any unnecessary noise, such as singing, whistling, or reading aloud. Capt. Bennett determined to overcome this difficulty by getting a few of the boys together, joining our hands in a circle around the wardens or any guards that might be near, and singing such songs as "The Old Cow Crossed the Road," or "Grasshopper Sitting on a Tatervine," etc. This seemed to take all right and met with no objections from the guards. We were also to make as much noise as possible while making breast pins, rings, etc. With our plans matured for the future, and in our imagination again breathing the air of liberty, we betook ourselves to different points of the prison, and in due course of time ate our supper and were locked up in our cells for the night, where we further planned for the future.

WORK BEGINS

Nov. 2nd. We thought it better to keep separated this morning and not allow more than two together at any one time. We now had two of the table knives, secured, I think, by Bennett and McGee. We put the two edges together and by striking them with a poker managed to make saws of them, which were to be used in cutting the cement mortar. They were of soft iron, driven into a block of pine or poplar wood handle. Capt. Hines swept his own cell that morning and so did one or two others, as we thought it best to do so. At half past eleven o'clock we went to dinner, when I managed to procure another knife, making the third one now in our possession, besides the pocket knives, which we thought to be sufficient with which to commence work.

Capt. Sheldon and myself went to Capt. Hines' cell, No. 20, and on that evening we made a beginning. My recollection is that we worked all that evening, but at night could scarcely tell what had been done. The cement or concrete proved to be harder than ordinary rock. Our knives were of soft metal and made but little impression on the floor, consequently Capt. Taylor had not much more than his vest pocket full of rubbish to dispose of. Yet we felt that we had made an excellent beginning. Capt. Hines was at his post all the while, keeping a sharp lookout lest some intruder should step in unawares.

Nov. 3rd. Bennett and McGee went on duty, while Taylor, Sheldon and myself stayed out in the hall, doing our best to entertain the guards and officers so as to keep them from cell No. 20. Strange to say the guards knew every prisoner so perfectly that they would miss any of us if we were absent from the crowd more than an hour at a time. Therefore, at first we had to be released from work frequently, so that we could make our appearance in the hall where we could be seen by them. But not so towards the close, because we all seemed to be so well contented and had given the wardens so little trouble, mixed with a good deal of "taffy," that they believed us to be resigned to our fate. All things considered, our day's work was very satisfactory.

Nov. 4th. The size of the hole which we cut in the cement I suppose was 14 inches square, though I never measured it. We got through the cement that day. Everything passed off quietly with no changes made in our arrangements, except that Taylor proposed to carry the straw out of Hines' bed-tick, burn it in the stove, and fill the tick with the brick, mortar, stone, etc.. We also concluded that one was enough to work at a time, as more would be in the way and impede the progress, and that also one would not be as likely to arouse suspicion as would more.

Nov. 5th. We began work as usual. It was but a short time until we had reached the arch, but we still had no idea how far it was to the air chamber. We made no new discoveries until late in the afternoon, at which time I was at work, when my knife slipped through the joint of mortar between two arched brick. I knew then that it would be no difficult job to reach the air chamber. Now came the exciting time with me. I wanted the pleasure of getting under that floor first. I cut and sawed the mortar from between three of these brick as rapidly as possible, lifted them out and then took one of the loose ones and knocked several others through to the ground, by striking them on the end. I then had a hole large enough for a small man to go through. I ventured down into this hole. I think it was the darkest place I ever saw before; it was about 4 feet or 4 1/2 feet to the ground. I could see nothing. I called to Captain Taylor, who was the only one who knew that I had gotten through, to bring me a candle. I lighted it and soon found out the full extent of the air chamber. At the west end it was about 18 inches from the arch to the floor, while at the east end it was not less than 12 feet.

There seemed to have been a room cut out of these for some purpose, but no door or entrance to it except a large air grate in the end wall. I could see no entrance to this chamber except the hole we had cut, and this air grate, the latter being stopped up with plank outside, which cut off all light. I had now seen all that there was to be seen underneath the floor, and thought it best to report the same to General Morgan and the boys. It is useless to try to describe my feelings while beneath the floor, as I thought of the near approach of our deliverance. I leave this to the imagination of the reader. I came out again into the light and started to Gen. Morgan's cell. He was engaged in talking to some of his men in the hall, but left them and followed me and invited me to take a seat and said, "Captain, what is the news?" I told him that I had been out reconnoitering. When he asked me what I meant by that I replied: "I have been all under this building." He slapped me on the shoulder and said, "Captain, you are a hell-fired liar." After describing things the best I could I proposed that he walked down to cell No. 20, lift up the black carpet sack, which we kept over the hole, and see for himself. He did so and was satisfied with the result. The brick and mortar was taken from the bed and thrown into the air chamber where there was plenty of room for it.

Nov. 6th. We were not able to understand why the plank was against the air grate, and the ventilation and light cut off from the chamber. I was determined to find out, because I thought that would be the next place for us to commence work, as at that point we would have only to cut through one wall or take out the air grate. I proposed when we went out to the wash trough, (to wash our faces) that we should learn the cause of this obstruction. It was not long until we were marched to the wash trough, and while some were washing, two or three of us sauntered about the yard in the direction of the end wall, above mentioned, and to our disgust found hundreds of bushels of coal piled against this wall and air grate. I saw at once that if we removed the grate that the coal would come down on us in an avalanche . It was, therefore, necessary to find some other place to begin work .

We began cutting through the cell wall. The first rock which we attempted to get out was an odd shaped one, with the larger end back in the wall, with a sharp point next to us; it gave us much trouble; it required three day's work to get it from its place.

Nov. 10th. Capt. Taylor had not been well since the 6th; Sheldon, Bennett, Magee and myself had been doing the work. These walls being so thick, we were compelled to cut in the face a space six or seven feet wide so that we might have an opening on the opposite side large enough for a man to go through. During the 11th nothing of importance transpired, but on the 12th the whole thing came near being a failure. Before commencing the work we agreed upon a system of signals by which we were to be governed. The bed prop was again to be brought into use. On tap with this on the floor was to notify those at work to come out and let others take their places. Two taps was a signal for dinner and was usually given a half an hour before time for eating. Three taps was the signal of danger and we were to come out as quickly as possible when this was given.

By some oversight on this day, those whose duty it was to give me the signal for dinner failed to do so. The others were called into line and marched into the dining hall, leaving me in the air chamber. Gen. Morgan made some excuse for not going to dinner and as soon as they all passed out of the gate he gave me the alarm signal. I came out as quickly as possible. They had missed me at roll call at dinner and Scott came on a hunt for me. I had just time to get out and brush my clothes when I heard him ask the General, who was standing between the gate and the cell, "Where is Capt. Hockersmith?" The General replied, "I left him lying upon my bed a few moments ago complaining of not being well. I had missed him and I came to look him up. Let's go up into my cell and see if he is there. " As soon as they got far enough beyond, that I could get there without detection, I went into it and covered myself up in bed. I saw that I would have to feign sickness which I did the best I could. When Scott found that I was not in Gen. Morgan's cell, he immediately came to mine and found me in bed and inquired as to my disease. He seemed satisfied, and as he left I asked him to bring me a little sick diet. In a short time he sent me some nice toasted bread , stewed chicken, and a cup of tea. I remained in my cell until 4 p.m., when the doctor came in and left me some medicine, which as soon as he left, I threw in the stove. No work was done that afternoon.

Nov. 13th found me still in the sick list, though improving rapidly. Some of the boys were at work under the floor. The doctor came in again and left some more medicine, which went into the stove to keep company with yesterday's stuff. It cured me and soon I went down to work again and found Bennett, Sheldon, and Magee had done well. This day we completed the journey through the first wall.

On the 14th of November we began digging the ditch from the cell wall to the outer wall of the main building, which was a distance of twenty feet. The first eighteen inches of this was loose dirt, made so by filling the trenches of the foundation walls. We supposed that the digging of the ditch would be an easy job, judging from the first foot and a half. But we soon discovered our mistake, for after getting through this stratum of loose dirt we came to a hard, tough clay, which did not yield very readily to our knives. I procured an additional knife, made by a convict out of an old razor blade; it proved to be the best tool for digging that we had been able to secure. I sharpened the end of it on a brick, and thus formed a kind of chisel of it. Capt. Taylor managed to get a shovel from a convict who was wheeling in coal, but we could only use the shovel in the loose dirt after we had digged it out with our knives. The ground was too hard, and the ditch or hole too small to use it as a spade.

After we had gone some four or five feet into the ditch, Capt. Taylor brought us a box 8x10 inches square and 8 inches deep. It had been sent filled with provisions to some of the boys. In the box we bored a hole with our pocket knives, tied a rope to it, made of a piece of bed ticking, and with the stick used to prop our beds we would push the box back into the ditch, where it would be filled by the man who was at work. When full it would be hauled out and emptied into the air chamber.

On the 17th of November Capt. Bennett was reported as not being able to work, on account of having blistered his hands; that left Sheldon, Magee and myself to complete the work, though Bennett sat at the mouth of the hole and drew out the dirt and emptied it. We were just seven days in cutting this ditch, which was in size 18 inches wide, 3 feet high and 12 feet long. One day while engaged in this work I came near being caught. I had traded one of the convicts out of a prison cap, which was made of the same material as their clothing. I wore it while at work to keep the dirt out of my hair. One day while at work our candles gave out, and I went up to get a fresh supply, and in the hurry forgot that I had on the prison cap; but fortunately the man from whom I had gotten it was sweeping the hall immediately in front of the cell I was going out of. He noticed the cap and told me to take it off, which I did, and threw it back into the cell without attracting any further notice. Had this been discovered by the officers, I would have been sent to the dungeon for my indiscretion. I secured my candles and went back to work. I think we used something near nine pounds of candles while engaged in this underground work. We had the privilege of buying them, provided we paid for them ourselves.

By the 21st of November we had completed nearly all the underground work except cutting through one wall. There had been no effort made to get the cell doors open as yet. Taylor and myself went to remind Capt. Hines of his promise. We found him in General Morgan's cell, and reminded him of his promise. He replied that it was impossible for him to get the doors open. The General then asked what was to be done. I proposed that we cut a hole through the floors of each one of our cells, proposing that we work up from underneath. I had made the same proposition to Taylor and Bennett before. They at once approved the plan, and seemed to be relieved.

We worked four days getting through the outer wall and cutting four feet up the wall toward the top of the ground, leaving about two feet to cut after other work was completed. We then went to work cutting through our cell floors. On the 25th I had another conversation with Gen. Morgan. He inquired as to how we were progressing. I told him that in two days more of the work would be completed. He expressed surprise at the progress we had made. He then proposed to me that if we made our escape and that if I would go with him to Richmond that he would give me $10,000 in gold. I thanked him, of course, but told him that it was freedom and not money that I was after. He replied: "That makes no difference; you must have the money." Capts. Bennett and Taylor were present at the time, and one of them – Bennett, I think – made the statement: "We never would have gotten through these arches and walls had it not been for Capt. Hockersmith, or some other brick-layer." The General sanctioned what was said. He also proposed to give me $50 or $100 to anyone in the first range of cells who would exchange cells with him the night we were to make the escape. The arrangement was effected with his brother, Col. Dick Morgan, and on the night of the escape they exchanged cells.

Sheldon, Magee and myself worked faithfully on the 26th and 27th, and just about completed the work of cutting through the other six floors. Sheldon and Magee cutting three of them their own and Col. Dick Morgan's – while I cut three – Capts. Taylor, Bennett and my own. We did not cut quite .through the six inches of concrete, but just nearly enough so that by a stroke of the foot from the top it would be broken through. The first hole made was under the bed in cell No. 20, the one through which we entered the air chamber, while the others were under the 15-inch plank which lay in front of the beds. In estimating the place to work up through from the bottom, it was only necessary to get the width of the cells and the thickness of the partition walls. Again we brought into use the bed prop, using it as a measuring pole.

On the next page is a roughly drawn diagram of the cell in which we worked, showing the cement and arches we cut through; also the ditch and two stone walls we cut through. The diagram represents cell No.

20, although it was cell No. 1 with end wall taken out, showing the end of it, and also ends of the air chamber. Also back of the bed with the wall taken away, giving a view of floor under the floor:

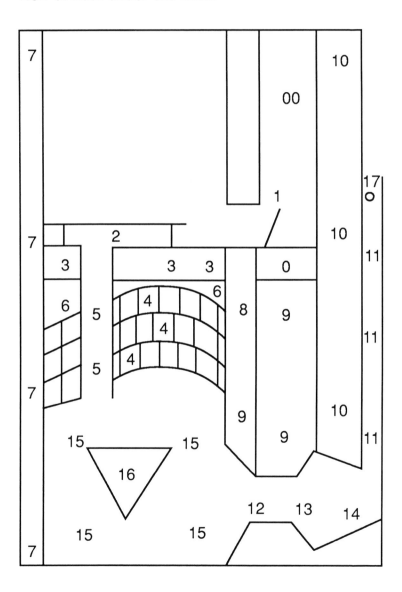

No. 0—Hall floor.

No. 00—Hallway.

No. 1—Doorway to cell.

No. 2—Bed stead.

No. 3—Concrete floor.

No. 4—Arches.

No. 5—Hole cut through to air chamber.

No. 6—Filling between arch and concrete.

No. 7—Wall between convicts and prisoners.

No. 8—Wall of prison cells.

No. 9—Between outer and inner walls.

No. 10—Outer wall.

No. 11—Hole digged upward as escape.

No. 12—Opening made from air chamber.

No. 13—Tunnel from wall to wall.

No. 14—Cut through outer wall.

No. 15—Air chamber.

No. 16—Rock removed from No. 11.

No. 17—Where we came out from under the prison.

Several parties had helped us in various ways. Capt. C. H. Morgan made our rope by tearing up a bed tick and plaiting it into a rope sufficiently large and strong to hold the weight of any ordinary man. Everything was now ready for us to make the attempt. Liberty was just before us; in a short time we should bid farewell to prison and prison rules. It had been determined that we should leave on the night of the 27th, just after the guard made his midnight round; but just

125

before we were locked up in our cells all agreed that the night was too light to make the attempt.

We had formed our plans to elude the watch. It was the custom of the night guard to examine the cells three times during the night—once at 10 o'clock, then at 12, again at 3. The guard carried with him what I call a coffee-pot lamp – that is a lamp with a spout to it – and as he approached the cell door, if he saw no one therein by the dim light, he would stick the spout through the bars and throw the light upon the bed. We knew that we should have to resort to some means to deceive him. It was agreed that we would always, if possible, have our heads covered up when he came, and in the event he stuck the spout in, to throw off the cover as if frightened. By this means he came to believe that we slept with our heads covered. So the night we escaped we stuffed our drawers and undershirts with straw taken from the beds, and after he had made his midnight round we covered the stuffed clothes up in bed and slid down into the air chamber.

It was agreed that on the night of the 28th we should make the start. The understanding was that Taylor should go down into the air chamber first and knock on the thin cement as a signal for us to go down. I followed him to complete the hole to the top of the ground, which work perhaps required some twenty or thirty minutes. I went up into the yard and found all quiet. It was then raining slowly, though it had been raining hard just before. The guards and their dogs had all gone under shelter. I went back and reported. Our rope was ready, with a good grab-hook made of a bent poker. We all now marched out into the yard. After getting there we found an inner wall about 12 feet from the main wall. That wall was only 20 feet high, while the other one was 25 feet high. This lower wall had in the end a slat gate which was not less than 12 feet high. The gate had a brace or two nailed on it. Taylor climbed up on the braces to the top of the gate, tied a rock to the end of the rope, threw it over the wall, let it swing down until he could reach through the gate, caught the end and tied it. The rope was made with loops, which made the climbing an easy matter. After we had gotten to the top of the lower wall we then had only five feet more to climb to get on top of the 25-foot wall.

We jumped on that, went round to the sentinel box or stand fronting the railroad, fastened our rope to an iron rod near the guardhouse, and after changing our clothing, we went down the rope to the ground. Gen. Morgan left his carpet-sack; Taylor and myself went back into the yard and got it. We were now outside the prison walls forever, and were bidding adieu to Columbus. We then separated for awhile. Bennett and myself agreed to travel together, Gen. Morgan and Hines were paired, Taylor and Sheldon together and Magee by himself. Bennett and myself went to the depot and procured tickets to Cincinnati. Gen Morgan had given me $7.00, and I already had about the same amount. After procuring our tickets we took seats in the coach. It was but a few minutes when Morgan and Hines came in. We pretended to be asleep until the train moved off. They ran near enough to the prison walls for us to see our rope swinging in the breeze. Gen. Morgan took his seat by the side of a Federal Colonel. I know not what passed between them, except a bottle of brandy, of which they both partook. Not long after that Morgan remarked that he saw two of his old Kentucky friends sitting just ahead of them, and that he wished to speak to them. He came where we were, shook hands with us, and after talking a moment went back to his seat by the Colonel. We said nothing more to him until we reached Cincinnati. Bennett and myself were standing on the platform when he came out where we were, and told us that he and Hines were going to jump off, and insisted that we do the same. I told him that we had purchased omnibus tickets for Covington, and that we would cross the river that way. He thought that if we went to the depot we would be captured. He bade us goodbye and jumped off.

Bennett and I remained in Covington until 11 o'clock a.m., let ourselves be known to a 15-year-old clerk, who gave us our breakfast and got us out of the city. We went to Owen county and after gathering corn for two or three weeks we left there and came to Hopkins county. I left Capt. Bennett sick near Ashbysburg, on Green river, and came to Madisonville. I remained at home two nights and one day, when I again took up my line of march, made my way to the Confederate army, was again captured, made my escape, to be the third time a captive of war, and the third time made my escape.

Forty years have passed since these stirring times, and a majority of those who went into that struggle now lie beneath the sod of the valley. The brave General Morgan did not live to see the close of the struggle or witness the failure of the "Lost Cause." A nobler, truer, or braver man than he never led men to battle.

The memory of this gallant soldier and his daring deeds are embalmed in the hearts of those who stood by him amid the trials and duties of war.

For my comrades who shared with me the toils and privations of a prison life, I have nothing but the kindest feeling, and pray that when the last trump shall sound that each and every one of them may have on the armor of salvation and all be happy throughout eternity.

Forty years have come and gone since the day I escaped.

Most of the men who fought in either army have crossed over the river and are now on the other side. I am still left and am enjoying life as well as most men of my age. The Lord has been good to and has blessed me in many ways. As I am coming down to the end of life, I can lay my hand upon my heart and say, no bitterness rankles there against any one who may have fought on the opposite side from that which I espoused. May the good Lord bless us all and may we all meet in the happy beyond where wars are heard of no more forever, is the prayer of a Johnny Reb.

L. D. Hockersmith

AN INDORSEMENT
NASHVILLE, TENN., 20, 1899

I wish to state I have carefully read and examined Captain L. D. Hockersmith's account of General Morgan and his companions escape from the Ohio State Penitentiary and find it to be a correct and impartial statement and account.

Capt. J. C. Bennett

P.S. I also authorize Captain Hockersmith to attach my name to said account whenever he desires to republish it.

Epilogue
To Part Two

In Hines' article, "Morgan and His Men Escape from Prison," published in the January 1891 issue of *Century* Magazine, he wrote that he discovered the dry cell floor, had the idea of the escape, and presented it to General Morgan.

In Duke's original 1867 edition of his "History of Morgan's Calvary," he stated that Capt. Hockersmith was "another of the projectors of the plan." But in his 1909 edition, Duke wrote, "Several plans were considered and abandoned, and at length one devised by Capt. Hines was adopted." But then, in a footnote, Duke added, "Captain L. D. Hockersmith of the Tenth Kentucky claims to have originated the plan of escape, and I believe that he and Hines simultaneously conceived it. He would make no claim he did not think just. He had more to do than anyone with its practical execution." (page 356)

The eminent Morgan historian and author, Professor James A. Ramage wrote*, "I think it is possible that several of the officers noticed the dry floor in the cells above the air shaft. It is possible that, from their own personal view, each one believed that the air shaft-tunnel escape was his idea."

My own views coincide with Dr. Ramage's hypothesis. But whosoever's ideas guided the escape, it was truly the most incredible prison escape of the Civil War.

W. Fred Conway

---

* Letter to the author dated January 28, 1994

Index

INDEX

Bibliography

CONWAY, W. FRED
Corydon - The Forgotten Battle of the Civil War
FBH Publishers, 1991

DUKE, BASIL W.
A History of Morgan and His Raiders
The University Press of Kentucky 1985

EDISON, H. THOMAS
John Hunt Morgan and His Raiders
The University Press of Kentucky 1985

HOLLAND, CECIL FLETCHER
Morgan And His Raiders
The Macmillan Co., 1942

HORAN, JAMES D.
Confederate Agent - A Discovery in History
Crown Publishers, Inc., 1954

KELLER, ALLAN
Morgan's Raiders
The Bobbs-Merril Co., Inc., 1961

RAMAGE, DR. JAMES A.
John Hunt Morgan's Escape
From the Ohio State Penitentiary
Civil War Quarterly Volume X

RISING, CLARA
In The Season of the Wild Rose
Villard Books, 1986

About the Author

Fred Conway is holding a rare book about Morgan's Raid, originally owned by the grandson of Col. Basil Duke, Morgan's second in command, as well as his brother-in-law.

W. Fred Conway, Sr., a writer and historian by avocation and an industrialist by vocation, has made an intensive study of the illustrious career of Civil War Brigadier General John Hunt Morgan.

Conway, a former fire chief, and a life-long fire buff, maintains a museum of antique fire apparatus and equipment at the Conway Enterprises Building in New Albany, Indiana. Other of his books include histories of vintage firefighting equipment.

He is a graduate of Duke University, with majors in English and music. He and his wife Betty live in Floyds Knobs, Indiana and Naples, Florida.

.

Other Books In This Series

- **Corydon — The Forgotten Battle Of The Civil War**
  By W. Fred Conway
  Only two "Official" Civil War battles were fought on northern soil — Gettysburg, and . . . Corydon. Includes the bizarre Ohio River crossing of 2,000 Rebels on captured steamboats.

- **The Ruthless Exploits Of Admiral John Winslow — Naval Hero Of The Civil War**
  By Paul Ditzel
  His great-grandfather had captured Bluebeard The Pirate, but Winslow sent to the bottom another buccaneer whose depredations made Bluebeard's look trifling by comparison.

- **Quantrill — The Wildest Killer Of The Civil War**
  By Paul Ditzel
  Armed with his own personal "death list," the Confederate sadist and plunderer, William Clarke Quantrill, left in his wake dead Union soldiers who had tried to surrender.

If not available at your favorite bookstore,
please order direct.